A Mother's Treasury
of Prayers ❧

A Mother's Treasury of Prayers ✤

Prayers and Blessings for
Your Children, Your Husband,
Your Home, and for
Every Occasion

Ronda De Sola Chervin

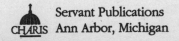
CHARIS

Servant Publications
Ann Arbor, Michigan

Charis Books is an imprint of Servant Publications especially
designed to serve Roman Catholics.

Scripture references, unless otherwise noted, are taken from the
New Revised Standard Version of the Bible, copyright 1989, by the
Division of Christian Education of the National Council of the
Churches of Christ in the United States of America and are used
by permission. All rights reserved.

Published by Servant Publications
P.O. Box 8617
Ann Arbor, Michigan 48107

Cover and text design by Diane Bareis

   95 96 97 98 10 9 8 7 6 5 4 3 2

Printed in the United States of America
ISBN 0-89283-851-5

Library of Congress Cataloging-in-Publications Data

Chervin, Ronda
    A mother's treasury of prayers : prayers and blessings for
your husband, your home, and for every occasion / Ronda De
Sola Chervin.
         p.   cm.
    "Charis Books."
    Includes bibliographical references and index.
    ISBN 0-89283-851-5
    1. Mothers--Prayer-books and devotions--English.   2.
Mothers-- Religious life.   3. Catholic Church--Prayer[books
and devotions--English.   I. Title.
BV4847.C48 1995
242'.8431--dc20
                                              94-37050
                                              CIP

Contents

Introduction ❧

I am the mother of three children who have walked on this earth and many miscarried ones who I hope went straight to heaven. I am also a grandmother to four beautiful grandchildren so far. In *A Mother's Treasury of Prayers,* I hope to be making contact with other Christian mothers who are seeking ways to bring to God in prayer the feelings in their hearts and the thoughts of their minds as they live through various phases of mothering.

From my own experience I know that whereas some of our motherly stirrings are of praise and gratitude, others are heavy with sorrow, frustration, irritation, exhaustion, bewilderment, and sometimes hateful resentment. Yet I also know from a long life as a mother—first of babies and finally of adult children—that every emotion is transformed for the good by coming to the Lord, to his mother, and to the angels and saints for help.

As I offer you my book of prayers for mothers I have a slight worry. I picture a mother who lifts her heart to God in prayer in quite simple ways, and I wonder: Will she come even closer to the Lord through the prayers I have selected—or might she do harm to this relationship by forcing herself to recite prayers against the leadings of the Spirit?

It is certainly not my intention to stifle the Spirit. Rather, I hope that some of the prayers I have selected will become freely chosen favorites of your own. Also, in cases where the style of a prayer does not suit your way of communing with God, some insight in the content of the prayer may start you off on your own meditative reflections.

When selecting prayers from the past which are very well known, I have kept the use of "thee" and "thou." In the case of lesser-known prayers I have taken the liberty of changing such words to contemporary usage by substituting "you."

One last comment. This book is a selection of prayers I have gathered from cards, leaflets, books of prayer; some I have composed myself or asked friends to write. But however lovely or insightful I have found these prayers to be, I never want to make it seem that they equal in value the formal prayer of the Church that is enunciated each day at all Masses and in the liturgy of the hours. It is only because these classical liturgical prayers are readily available elsewhere that I am not including them in this book.

In fact, like many other Catholic mothers, I have found that the most important and satisfying way of praying for my children is to offer their needs to God at Mass. Receiving Jesus in Holy Communion has always given me such strength that I even found a way to participate in daily Mass when my twins were one and a half (for me, the most difficult time of being a mother) and too wild to sit still for thirty minutes. I used to stroll them over to the church just in time for the consecration, then I wheeled them around outside and returned for Holy Communion!

Of course, pressing duties will often prevent mothers from attending Mass on a daily basis. But those who make it their highest priority to do so whenever possible will find that it is an unfailing source of grace for all the challenges of motherhood. (For prayers that pertain to the Mass, see chapter two.)

As you read *A Mother's Treasury of Prayers,* here is my special prayer for you.

Blessing Prayer for Mother's Day

God of Love,
listen to this prayer.

God of Holy People,
of Sarah, Ruth and Rebekah;
God of holy Elizabeth, mother of John,
of holy Mary, Mother of Jesus,
bend down your ear to this request
and bless the mother(s) of our family.

Bless her with the strength of your Spirit,
she who taught her child(ren)
how to stand and how to walk.

Bless her with the melody of your love,
she who has shared how to speak,
how to sing and how to pray to you.

Bless her with a place at your eternal
dinner table,
she who has fed and nurtured
the life that was formed within her
while still helpless but embraced in her love.

Bless her today,
now, in this lifetime,
with good things, with health.

Bless her with joy, love, laughter,
and pride in her children
and surround her with many good friends.

May she who carried life in her womb
be carried one day to your divine embrace:
there, for all eternity,
to rejoice with her family and friends.

This blessing and all graces, we pray,
descend upon the mother of our family:
in the name of the Father,
and of the Son,
and of the Holy Spirit.
Amen!

Ronda De Sola Chervin
Feast of Our Lady of Lourdes
February 11, 1994

Editor's note: Unless otherwise noted, all prayers and reflections have been written by the author or compiled from commonly used prayers of the Church.

Could you not watch one hour with Me

Angel's Prayer

With the Blessed Sacrament suspended in the air, the angel at Fatima prostrated himself, and recited this prayer:

O Most Holy Trinity,
Father, Son and Holy Spirit,
I adore Thee profoundly.
I offer Thee the most precious
Body, Blood, Soul and Divinity
of Jesus Christ, present in all
the tabernacles of the world, in
reparation for the outrages,
sacrileges and indifference by
which He is offended.
By the infinite merits of the
Sacred Heart of Jesus and the
Immaculate Heart of Mary,
I beg the conversion of
poor sinners.

Chapter One ❧

A Catholic Mother's Guide to Daily Spirituality

Lord,
may I be wakeful at sunrise
to begin a new day for you;
cheerful at sunset
for having done my work for you;
thankful at moonrise and under starshine
for the beauty of your universe.
And may I add what little may be in me
to add to your great world.

The Abbot of Greve

ll mothers experience both joy and stress in their lives. Even as they rejoice over the goodness and beauty of each child, mothers also groan under the burden of their daily tasks, fearing that they will simply collapse under the strain. To live each day in a loving way, mothers have great need of constant prayer not only for their children but for themselves.

In this chapter you will find a variety of prayers that are suitable for every day. Some of these prayers lend themselves to silent personal use. Others are especially good for praying aloud—so that your children will pick up the idea that God is ever present in the home, ready to listen.

❧ Morning Prayers ❧

Thank You, God, for this new day,
for the life you are giving each member of my family:
Thank you for (name each member of the immediate
    family, not forgetting yourself).
Bless each one of us
with the strength and health we need to serve you today,
with the joy we need not to give in to discouragement,
    anger, or boredom,
with the protection we need against physical and
    moral danger,
with the love we need to give hope to those we meet.

Dear God,
I want to respond to everything
beautiful you want to bring to my attention today,
and to transmit my joy to my children.

Like the poet William Blake I want to be able to
"see a world in a grain of sand
And a heaven in a wild flower,
to hold infinity in the palm of my hand
and eternity in an hour."[1]

Anonymous

Come, Holy Spirit,
and teach me
how to awaken
not with tired grumbling
but with song and praise.

O Lord,
thou knowest how busy I must be this day;
if I forget thee,
do not forget me.

Sir Jacob Astley
from *A Book of Everyday Prayer*

"My God,
I desire to do
and to endure
everything today
for love of you."

✣

St. Bernadette of Lourdes

❧ Prayers Throughout ❧ the Day

Daily Invocation of the Holy Spirit

Come, Holy Spirit,
Fill the hearts of your faithful,
and kindle in them the fire of your love.
Send forth your Spirit
and we shall be created,
and you will renew the face of the earth.

Holy Spirit,
brooding over the formless world
and bringing order out of chaos:
fashion our spirit.

Holy Spirit,
inspiration of the prophets,
bestower of wisdom and knowledge:
speak to our spirit.

Holy Spirit, knowing the deep things of God:
move within the depths of our being.

Holy Spirit,
consuming fire:
burn away all that is not holy.

Holy Spirit,
blessed warmth and consolation:
inspire us with courage and love.

O Holy Spirit,
life and light of the Church,
give us thoughts higher than our own thoughts,
and prayers better than our own prayers,
and powers beyond our own powers,
that we may love and live,
imitating Jesus Christ,
our Lord and Savior. Amen.

from *Prayers for Daily and Occasional Use*

The Angelus

Catholics most often say this prayer at noon but also at six in the morning and the evening. Busy mothers may be able to pause and recite the Angelus at one of these times. It is a much-loved way to remember to whom we belong and to what we aspire, in the very midst of the daily routines of life and work that tend to distract us.

The angel of the Lord declared unto Mary,
And she conceived of the Holy Spirit.
Hail Mary...
Behold the handmaid of the Lord.
Be it done unto me according to your word.
Hail Mary...
And the Word was made flesh,
And dwelt among us.
Hail Mary...
Pray for us, O holy Mother of God.
That we may be made worthy of the promises of Christ.

Let us pray:

Pour forth, we beseech you, O Lord,
Your grace into our hearts;
that as we have known the incarnation
   of Christ, your Son,
by the message of an angel,
so by his passion and cross we may be brought
to the glory of his Resurrection.
Through the same Christ, our Lord. Amen.

Novenas

Novenas are formal prayers said for nine days for a particular intention. It usually takes about ten minutes to say such a prayer which includes Scripture, reflections, and aspirations. A mother could pray for the needs of a particular child or for some urgent need of her own.

There are many different novenas asking for the intercession of the Sacred Heart, the Immaculate Heart of Mary, St. Joseph, and other saints. Some Catholics go from one novena to the next throughout the year; they find that these prayers help them to avoid brooding over their problems and to confide their anxieties to God through his friends, with many good results.

Here is a beautiful novena in honor of the Holy Spirit to be prayed for nine days before Pentecost.

Come, O Holy Spirit, fill the hearts of thy faithful,
and enkindle in them the fire of thy love.
Send forth thy Spirit, and they shall be created.
And thou shalt renew the face of the earth.

Let us pray.

O God, who by the light of the Holy Spirit, did instruct
the hearts of the faithful, grant that in the same Spirit we
may be truly wise, and ever rejoice in his consolation.
Through Christ our Lord. Amen.

Act of Contrition. *"O God, be merciful to me a sinner." I*
am sincerely sorry for all the sins, faults, and infidelities
of my life because they offend thee, my chief Benefactor

and sovereign God. I firmly resolve by the grace of the Holy Spirit to sin no more. Amen.

Prayer for Humility. *O God, who resists the proud and bestows thy grace on the humble, grant us the virtue of true humility of which thine only begotten Son showed to the faithful an example in himself; that we may never provoke thee to anger by our pride, but rather receive through humility the gift of thy grace. Through the same Jesus Christ our Lord. Amen.*

Reflection. *The Blessed Virgin Mary taught us how to respond to the inspiration of divine grace. When the angel Gabriel announced to her: "The Holy Spirit shall come upon thee and the power of the Most High shall overshadow thee, and therefore, also, the Holy, which shall be born of thee shall be called the Son of God," Mary answered: "Be it done unto me according to thy word."*

Act of Consecration to the Holy Spirit. *O Divine Redeemer, who said: "I will ask the Father, and he will grant you another Advocate to be with you for all time, the Spirit of Truth. I consecrate myself to the eternal Spirit of God. Aspiration of love, proceeding from the Father and the Son, alert me to be ever aware of thy indwelling; stimulate the eyesight of my soul to discern the unfailing light of divine grace. Adorable Holy Spirit, have compassion on the dullness of my mind and the weakness of my will. Illuminate and strengthen me to trample on temptation.*

Grant me the Spirit of Wisdom, the prevision to look to my last end by cooperating now with thy holy inspirations—all for the greater honor and glory of God; the Spirit of Understanding to deepen my grasp of eternal truths; the Spirit of Counsel to prudently choose the best way of pleasing God; the Spirit of Fortitude to stand up fearless in opposition to evil; the Spirit of Knowledge—self-inspection regarding my fidelity to God's laws and the duties of my state in life; the Spirit of Piety to enable me to prefer my Divine Lover and his will to earthly creatures; the Spirit of Fear of the Lord to realize the folly and ingratitude of defying my Lord and my God.

Kneeling before thee, O Divine Consoler, let me press to my heart the pierced feet of Jesus, look into his open side and trust in his Precious Blood channeled to my soul through the sacraments.

O Holy Spirit, enfold all mankind with thy sevenfold gifts. Keep me faithful unto death that I may win the crown of life. Amen.

Our Father, Hail Mary, Glory be...

The Rosary

For mothers, praying the holy rosary—either alone or with the family—is a popular way of turning to God. Many mothers carry a rosary around all day and pray the mysteries whenever they find a short period of time between duties. The comforting rhythm of moving one's fingers over the beads has a soothing effect on the harried. Many mothers also like to offer special prayers for each child before each mystery. (Instructions on how to pray the rosary can be found in every Catholic bookstore or by asking someone in the parish who prays it regularly.)

The Mercy Prayer.

The mercy prayer, or chaplet of divine mercy, has become popular among Catholics in recent years. It can be prayed using a rosary at any time, but many people like to offer it between three and four o'clock in the afternoon. Mothers might like to pray each decade for a child or other member of the family.

Using rosary beads, begin with an Our Father, Hail Mary, and Apostles' Creed. Then on the Our Father beads pray:

Eternal Father, I offer you the Body and Blood, Soul and Divinity of your dearly beloved Son, Our Lord Jesus Christ, in atonement for our sins and those of the whole world.

On the Hail Mary beads pray:

For the sake of his sorrowful Passion have mercy on us and on the whole world.

In conclusion say three times:

Holy God, Holy Mighty One, Holy Immortal One, have mercy on us and on the whole world.

The Memorare

Besides the rosary, the Memorare is perhaps the most beloved of all prayers asking for Mary's intercession. I used to find it difficult to say this prayer because I thought that the message in it about no one ever being left unaided by Mary meant that praying to her had infallible results. Gradually I came to see what it means: You will be helped, but not necessarily in the way you would choose. A prayer to get a certain job might lead to getting a different one that is better for you in the long run, or a prayer for healing might lead to finding the ultimate healing of being taken out of this world into the arms of Jesus.

Remember, O most gracious Virgin Mary, that never was it known that anyone who fled to your protection, implored your help, or sought your intercession was left unaided.

Inspired by this confidence, I fly to you, O Virgin of virgins, my mother. To you I come; before you I stand, sinful and sorrowful.

O Mother of the Word incarnate, despise not my petitions, but in your mercy, hear and answer me. Amen.

The Anima Christi

Soul of Christ, sanctify me.
Body of Christ, save me.
Blood of Christ, inebriate me.
Water from the side of Christ, wash me.
Passion of Christ, strengthen me.
O good Jesus, hear me.
Within your wounds hide me.
Separated from you let me never be.
From the malignant enemy, defend me.
At the hour of death, call me.
And close to you, bid me.
That with your saints I may be
Praising you, for all eternity. Amen.

Prayer to St. Michael

*St. Michael the Archangel, defend us in battle; be our
defense against the wickedness and snares of the devil.
May God rebuke him, we humbly pray; and do you, O
prince of the heavenly host, by the power of God, thrust
into hell Satan and the other evil spirits who prowl about
the world, seeking the ruin of souls. Amen.*

*Most Sacred Heart of Jesus,
have mercy on us* (repeat 3 times).

Prayer for Forgiveness

*Dear Jesus,
another day has passed
when I have not been a saint!*

*Terrible to count the ways I have failed.
I do not want to recall
the looks on the faces of my children
or my husband
when my anger, out of proportion as usual,
surprised them,
interrupting some small pleasure
they tried to seize outside the rhythm of my relentless
    demands!*

I do not want to recall
the look on my face
when I caught a glimpse of it
in the bathroom mirror
this afternoon,
so disgruntled and ungrateful
and peevish.

I do not want to recall
the hurt look on the face of a child
who wanted a few moments of undivided attention
which I would not give
because the voice at the end of the phone
was more attractive.

No, instead,
I want to recall
your face, Jesus,
full of patient long-suffering love
for me,
bidding me rest
and try again
tomorrow.

Confession of Powerlessness and Need for God

Dear God,
I am powerless
and my life is unmanageable
without your love and guidance.
I come to you tonight
because I believe that
you can restore and renew me
to meet my needs tomorrow
and to help me meet
the needs of my children.

Since I cannot manage my life or affairs,
I have decided to give them to you.
I put my life, my will,
my thoughts,
my desires and ambitions in your hands.
I give you each of my children.

I give you all of me:
the good and the bad,
the character defects and shortcomings,
my selfishness, resentments, and problems.

I know that you will work them out
in accordance with your plan.

Such as I am,
take and use me in your service.
Guide and direct my ways
and show me what to do for you.

I cannot control or change my children,
other family members or friends,
so I release them into your care
for your loving hands to do with as you will.
Just keep me loving and free from judging them.

If they need changing, God,
you'll have to do it; I can't.
Just make me willing and ready
to be of service to you,
to have my shortcomings removed,
and to do my best.

Help me to see how I have harmed others
and make me willing to make amends to them all.
Keep me ever mindful of thoughts and actions
that harm myself and others,
and which separate me from your light,
love and spirit.

And when I commit these errors,
make me aware of them
and help me to admit each one promptly.

I am seeking to know you better,
to love you more.
I am seeking the knowledge of your will for me
and the power to carry it out.

Anonymous

Aspirations and the Jesus Prayer

In addition to the longer or more formal prayers mentioned above, mothers can derive much strength for the day by turning to God in frequent, short prayers called aspirations. Catholics have long used spontaneous prayers such as these to offer to God their daily annoyances and crosses.

"I offer this pain for the souls in purgatory."

"I offer up this traffic jam for my son to get off drugs."

"Jesus, Mary, Joseph, I love you, save souls."

"I offer this housework for the ultimate salvation of each of my children."

Such prayers help us to avoid giving in to irritation, discouragement, and despair. They remind us that Jesus will unite our sufferings to his merits to use for the salvation of souls.

Aspiration prayers can punctuate the day of a mother with remembrance of God. They can also lead into a practice much loved in the Orthodox church and adopted by the Western church—the Jesus prayer, which consists in constantly praying the name of Jesus or the words, "Lord, Jesus Christ, have mercy on me, a poor sinner." Eventually the Jesus prayer can settle into the rhythm of one's breathing and enter into the heart in a way that is truly sanctifying.

Our Lady of Fatima suggests not only offering sufferings that come to us unbidden but also offering sacrifices of our own choosing: fasting, saying prayers or undertaking unpleasant tasks, for example. These can be offered especially for the salvation of sinners (including ourselves, of course!) and for the spiritual welfare of our families.

Prayers for the Family

O dear Jesus,
I humbly implore you to grant your special graces
to our family.
May our home be the shrine of peace, purity, love,
labor and faith.
I beg you, dear Jesus, to protect and bless all of us,
absent and present, living and dead.
O Mary,
loving Mother of Jesus, and our Mother,
pray to Jesus for our family,
for all the families of the world,
to guard the cradle of the newborn,
the schools of the young and their vocations.
Blessed Saint Joseph,
holy guardian of Jesus and Mary,
assist us by your prayers in all the necessities of life.
Ask of Jesus that special grace which he granted to you,

to watch over our home at the pillow of the sick
    and dying,
so that with Mary and with you,
heaven may find our family
unbroken in the Sacred Heart of Jesus. Amen.

Catholics United for the Faith

For a Spirit of Prayer in the Family

Come, Holy Spirit,
teach us how to pray
together as a family

so that we may honor God,
praise him,
listen to his word.

So that Jesus
may sweeten our relationships,
give us honesty in expressing our needs,
and help us to forgive each other
and support each other.

May our prayer together
make our home become a little church.

Anonymous

Prayer for My Marriage

*I call upon you,
Mary and Joseph,
and on those saints
who were happily married
to intercede for us.
May our marriage bond
be strengthened
through the graces of the sacrament.*

*May my husband and I
both grow together in the Spirit.
May our work in the world
be accomplished out of love for God
and never be an obstacle
to love in the family.*

*May the love between us
always be renewed in your grace,
dear Lord,
and overflow into our love
for our children.*

Prayer for a Loving Marriage

In the sacrament of marriage,
you bound us together in love.
Help us to overcome all strife,
all selfishness,
all resentment,
that our home
may be filled with love
and our children be happy now
and also when they are grown.

Grace Geist

Mary, Come and Live with Us

Come, O Mary, come and live in this house…
We welcome you with the joy of children.

Give to each of us
all the necessary spiritual graces
just as you brought them
to the house of Zachary.

Give us material graces
as you obtained for the newlyweds at Cana
the changing of water into wine.

Always keep sin far from us.
Be light, joy, and sanctity
as you were in the family of Nazareth.

Be here our Mother, Teacher, and Queen.
Increase in us:
faith, hope, and charity.
Infuse in us the spirit of prayer,
so that here,
together with you, Jesus,
Way, Truth, and Life
we may always live.

Rev. J. Alberione
(founder of the Daughters of St. Paul)

Prayer of Faith for Our Home

Almighty God,
You have called us to the holy state of matrimony
and have shared with us your gift of creation.
We thank you for making our love fruitful.

May we be worthy representatives
of you, dear Lord,
in forming our children
in your knowledge and love.

You have given us children,
Almighty God,
to teach in your ways
which will lead
to their eternal home of heaven.

May our children ever walk in
the ways of your commandments
and live according to
the teachings of your holy Catholic Church.

May our example, dear God,
be such as to inspire our children
to grow into the likeness
of your Son, Jesus Christ.

May we be firm but kind in discipline.
May we stand as one
united in authority
so as to be consistent.

May we never confuse
permissiveness with love.
May we teach our children
respect for your authority
in ourselves and
in all your representatives on earth.

May our home be as a Church,
for you, Lord Jesus Christ,
are present wherever two or three are gathered
together in your name.

May praises of God frequently
rise from the lips and hearts of our family
and may we all one day
be united in our eternal home. Amen.

Anonymous

House Blessing

May Christ be Ruler in our home for aye
Beginning now upon our Wedding Day.

May Christ's own Mother make her dwelling here,
To share each simple joy, to soothe each tear.

May Christ be king in all the hearts that stay
Beneath this roof of ours, both night and day.

These two, throughout our lives, our guests shall be;
Then we shall be their guest... eternally!

Sister Angela Clare Gorman, S.P.

Sometimes, a mother's prayers are the fruit of meditating on some words or sayings from the saints. This prayer was inspired by St. Margaret of Youville, a recently canonized mother and foundress of a religious order who lived in Canada in the eighteenth century.

Prayer to St. Margaret of Youville

*"All the wealth in the world
cannot be compared with the
happiness of living together happily united."
That is what you taught,
St. Margaret of Youville.*

*We ask you to pray for our family
that we may have the happiness today
of overcoming discord through loving kindness
    and forgiveness,
that we may end the day
happily united in the Heart of Jesus.*

For A Spirit of Love in Our Home

*God, make the door of this house
wide enough to receive all
who need human love and fellowship....*

Make its threshold smooth enough
to be no stumbling block
to children, nor to straying feet,
but rugged and strong enough
to turn back the tempter's power.

God, make the door of this house
the gateway to Thine eternal kingdom.

On the door of St. Stephen's in London

May We Be a Blessing, Lord

In your great mercy, O Lord,
grant that this may be a good day in this home.
Save us from becoming casual with each other.
Save us from lack of self-discipline.
Save us from discourtesy.
Bless any who shall come over our doorstep,
any who shall sit at our table,
or share talk with us
over the phone.

Let us use our home
and the treasured things we have
gathered about us
to give others joy.

Make us each discreet in our conversation,
and loving and loyal to each other.

And to you
we should give all the glory and praise. Amen.

Rita Snowden

In Time of Journeying and Separation from a Husband

O God, our Father,
beyond whose love and care we cannot drift,
bless (husband's name) *in his journeying today.*
Bring him in safety to his journey's end;
and let no ill befall him in body, mind, or spirit.

Grant that,
when we are separated from each other,
we may ever remember that,
though we are absent from one another,
we are still present with you.
And keep us true and faithful to each other
until we meet again
through Jesus Christ our Lord. Amen.

William Barclay
from *A Book of Everyday Prayer*

Prayer of Thanksgiving

I depend on you
for the eyes which miraculously camera the
    lovely world
you created for my service and delight
for my mind and the truth that must fill it
for my body and the food and light and water
    and air that keep it going
for friendship and love and books and music,
for the service of animals and the mercy of men
    and the gentleness of women
for health, your gift,
and sickness, often your greater gift,
for laughter and the sense of humor,
for the power to run and the instinct to create,
for the birth of children
    and the release from old age of gentle death
I depend upon you, dear Lord,
and the thought should make me deeply humble
    and wonderfully glad.

Daniel Lord

Night-time Blessing

Thank you, Jesus
for all the good moments of this day.
Thank you, Jesus,
for the strength to live this day.
Thank you, Jesus,
for the help of my loving husband.
Thank you, Jesus,
for the good things my children did.
Thank you, Jesus,
for the help of Mother Mary,
our angels and patron saints.

Give me a restful night
that I may arise refreshed.

Chapter Two ❧

Mass as a Source of Spiritual Strength

The Catholic Church teaches that there is no source of spiritual strength as great as Holy Mass because of the real presence of Christ in the Eucharist.

It makes sense, therefore, for mothers to try to go to Mass as often as possible. When the children are very little, some mothers do exchange baby-sitting to be able to participate in daily Mass at least every other day. Others bring their small children for as much of the Mass as they can sit through without disrupting the services.

❧ Prayer before Mass ❧

Whether for a daily or a weekly Mass, it is good to prepare yourself and the children by arriving early and focusing your mind on the meaning of the Mass and the special themes of the feast day or Sunday. You might say a simple prayer like this one:

My Jesus, I am so grateful that you wished to be so close to us through the sacrament of Holy Communion. Please send the Holy Spirit to open me to understand this mystery more and more so that I may find the strength I need from your holy Body and Blood to live the way of love you desire for me.

Some families prepare for Mass by praying over the readings beforehand and talking about how they apply to their own lives. It is also good to stay a few moments after Mass to thank Jesus for the great gift of his Body and Blood.

❧ Spiritual Communion ❧

Often a mother's schedule and responsibilities prevent her from attending daily Mass and receiving Holy Communion. In such situations, where you wish you could be receiving but cannot, you can make an act of spiritual communion. As a mother you might derive special comfort from offering your spiritual communion for one of your children. Here is an act of spiritual communion attributed to St. Francis of Assisi.

I believe that you, O Jesus,
are in the most holy Sacrament.
I love you and desire you.
Come into my heart.
I embrace you.
Oh, never leave me.
May the burning and most sweet power of your love,
O Lord Jesus Christ,
I beseech you,
absorb my mind
that I may die through love of your love,
who were graciously pleased
to die through love of my love.

❧ The Mystical Mass Prayer ❧

Composed by Father Luke Zimmer, SS.CC., the Mystical Mass prayer has been growing in popularity among Catholics. Many mothers find this prayer—which links their intercessory prayers to the Mass—particularly helpful. Not only is the prayer itself beautiful, but it can also help at-home mothers who may be feeling isolated from the rest of the world by expanding their horizons to the whole mystical body of Christ.

Eternal Father,
we offer to You,
through the Immaculate and Sorrowful Heart of Mary,
in the Holy Spirit,
the Body, Blood, Soul and Divinity
of Our Lord Jesus Christ,
in union with each Mass celebrated
today and every day until the end of time.

With Mother Mary, St. Joseph,
each angel and saint in Heaven,
each soul in Purgatory,
each person in the Body of Christ
and the family of God,
we offer each act of love,
adoration, praise and worship.

We offer each act of thanksgiving
for blessings, graces and gifts received.

We offer each act of reparation
for sins that have been,
are being,
and will be committed
until the end of time.
And we offer each act

of intercessory prayer.
We offer all these prayers
in union with Jesus in each Mass
celebrated throughout the world
until the end of time.

We stand before You, Triune God,
like the Prodigal Son asking to be accepted,
like the Publican asking for mercy and forgiveness,
like the Paralytic asking for healing and strength,
and like the Good Thief asking for salvation.

We consecrate ourselves and all of creation to You.

Eternal Father,
we ask You in the Name of Jesus,
through the power of His Precious Blood,
through His death on the Cross,
through His resurrection and ascension
to send forth the Holy Spirit upon all mankind.

Holy Spirit,
we ask for an outpouring of Your graces, blessings
    and gifts
upon those who do not believe, that they may believe;
upon those who are doubtful or confused,
    that they may understand;
upon those who are lukewarm or indifferent,
    that they may be transformed;
upon those who are constantly living in the state of sin,

that they may be converted;
upon those who are weak,
    that they may be strengthened;
upon those who are holy, that they may persevere.

We ask You to bless our Holy Father.
Give him strength and health
in mind, body, soul, and spirit.
Bless his ministry and make it fruitful.
Protect him from his enemies.

Bless each cardinal, bishop, priest,
brother, sister,
and all aspiring to the religious life,
especially (their names here)
and grant many the gift of a vocation
to the priesthood and religious life.

Bless each member of our families,
relatives and friends, especially (their names here).

Bless the poor, the sick,
the underprivileged, the dying
and all those in need ….

Bless those who have died
and are in the state of purification,
that they may be taken to heaven….

We offer to consecrate ourselves
and all creation to You,
Heart of Jesus, Mary and Joseph.

We ask you Mary and Joseph
to take us with all our hopes and desires.
Please offer them with Jesus
in the Holy Spirit
to our Heavenly Father,
in union with each Mass
offered throughout all time.

We consecrate ourselves to
Archangels Michael, Gabriel, and Raphael,
and each angel,
especially our Guardian Angel.
We ask in the Name of Jesus,
through our Mother Mary,
Queen of all Angels,
that You, O Heavenly Father,
send forth legions of angels to minister to us:

Archangel Michael with his legions
to ward off the attacks of the world,
the flesh and the devil;

Archangel Gabriel with his legions
to teach us that we may know
and do Your will,
and that they may help us to
catechize and evangelize;

Archangel Raphael with his legions
to heal our woundedness,
supply for our limitations,

and strengthen us in our weakness
to overcome demonic depression,
to give us joy in the spirit,
to protect us in our travels
and to supply all our needs.

Finally,
we ask for the gift of unconditional love,
that we can live the love-life which
was reflected in the Holy Family at Nazareth,
thus bringing about justice and peace
throughout the world. Amen. [2]

Chapter Three ❧

Prayers for Mothers of Infants

The most important person
on earth is a mother.
She cannot claim the honor
of having built Notre Dame Cathedral.
She need not.
She has built something more magnificent
than any cathedral—
a dwelling for an immortal soul,
the tiny perfection of her baby's body...
the angels have not been blessed
with such a grace.
They cannot share in
God's creative miracle
to bring new saints to heaven.
Only a human mother can.
Mothers are closer to God the Creator

than any other creature;
God joins forces with mothers
in performing this act of creation....
What on God's good earth
is more glorious than this: to be a mother?

Joseph Cardinal Mindszenty

The prospect of becoming a mother is a wonderful stimulus to prayer! Quite naturally it can lead to a deeper desire to be close to God—an openness that springs out of awe and wonder at the prospect of participating so intimately in the mystery of a new life.

Then, too, a mother-to-be has so many particular intentions on her mind. From the very beginning stages of praying for a child to the actual moment of birth, there is ample material to bring before the Lord—as is evident from the selection of prayers that follows.

❧ Before a Baby is Born ❧

Prayers to Conceive a Child

St. Gerard Majella is invoked as the patron saint of childbirth. Perhaps this is because his own birth was difficult and his life in danger, or because the Christ-child is said to have been his playmate as a boy, or because he loved children especially.

O good St. Gerard,
powerful Intercessor before God
and Wonderworker of our day,
I call upon you and seek your aid.

You who on earth
did fulfill God's designs,
help me to do
the holy Will of God.

Beseech the Master of Life,
from whom all paternity proceeds,
to render me fruitful in offspring,

That I may
raise up children to God
in this life
and heirs to the Kingdom of His Glory
in the world to come. Amen.

I thank you, God,
for my husband's love.
It is because we love each other so much
that we want so much to have
a little child to mirror our love.
It is you who gave us this great love;
now we beg you to crown our blessings
by sending us a baby.

Lord of Heaven and Earth
I invoke now the memory
of all the women in Scripture
who wished for a child
but had to wait a long time.

In the name of Sarah (Genesis 21:1-2),
in the name of the wife of Manoah (Judges 13:2-5, 24),
in the name of Hannah (1 Samuel 1:1-2:11),
in the name of Rebekah (Genesis 25:21),
in the name of Elizabeth (Luke 1:11-15, 24-25),

I beg you, God,
to send me a child
that I may be a fruitful wife
and a happy mother of children.

Quin Sherrer and **Ruthanne Garlock**
Adapted from *The Spiritual Warrior's Prayer Guide*

Prayer for a Mother with Child

O Almighty and Everlasting God,
who, through the operation of the Holy Spirit,
prepared the body and soul
of the glorious Virgin Mary
to be a worthy dwelling place
of thy Divine Son; and,
through the operation of the same Holy Spirit,
sanctified St. John the Baptist,
while still in his mother's womb;
hear the prayers of your humble servant
who implores you,
through the intercession of St. Gerard,
to protect me
amid the dangers of childbearing
and to watch over the child
with which you have deigned to bless me,
that it may be cleansed
by the saving water of Baptism and,
after a Christian life on earth,
it may with me attain
everlasting bliss in heaven.
Amen.

Adapted from *St. Gerard Guild*

Prayers for the Preborn

O Father in heaven
You are the Creator of life.
Protect all expectant mothers
and the babies they carry in their wombs.

We pray that those who suffer
from the evils of abortion
will be open to your infinite
mercy and love.

We ask for the conversion
of all who fail to respect
the gift of human life.

Heavenly Father,
guide our actions
to help restore in the hearts of all people
the sanctity of human life. Amen.

A baby is on the way, Lord,
and our hearts are filled
with ever-increasing delight
as we marvel at the awesome mystery
of being co-creators with you.

Even while we parents-to-be rejoice
in being recipients of your love
and the instruments of your will,

we regard with apprehension
this responsibility that is ours.
We feel so much
the need of relating more deeply to you.

We look forward with expectancy and joy
to the birth of our child.
As we cling more closely to one another,
we commit ourselves to you,
resting in the confidence
that this baby is in your embrace,
that you will care for our child and for us.

We pray that each of us and our child
may be your children
and your beloved servants forever.

Leslie and **Edith Brandt**
as quoted in *Draw Me*

Prayer for a Miscarried Baby

Flown like a bird into the arms of God?
Too good for his (her) feet to touch the ground?

But I wanted that baby so much, Lord!
Did you think I was not worthy to mother that baby?
Or was it your way to prevent
a baby with birth defects
from suffering in this world?

I feel very empty, Jesus.
Help me to accept your permissive will.
Help me to have courage to try again.
Help me to rejoice that this baby
does exist and will live
for all eternity
and that one day
I will see my baby
as a grown person
when my time on earth is over.

I offer the pain in my heart
that you may use it just as you wish
for your glory and honor.

Grace Geist

Prayer for a Stillborn Baby

St. Clotilda said: "I give thanks to Almighty God that he has not considered me unworthy to be the mother of a child admitted into the celestial kingdom. Having quitted the world in the white robe of his innocence, he will rejoice in the presence of God through all eternity."

We ask you, St. Clotilda,
to infuse in our suffering hearts
joy for the heavenly happiness of our baby,
so that we may be comforted,
and freed from all bitterness,
at the loss of this dear baby's
presence with us on earth.

Prayer for an Aborted Baby

*I come to you, my Jesus,
stricken with remorse
about the baby
whose face I never saw.*

*I didn't really believe in
your love when I did it.
I just knew I couldn't
handle it.
Couldn't handle
telling my parents,
my boyfriend's rejection.*

But now that I am a mother
and a woman who knows who you are,
I wonder about that aborted baby.
Where is he or she?

I feel your arms around me.
I see you pointing to your mother, Mary,
and showing me my babe
lying in her lap
with her tears
flowing like baptismal water.

Can you make me sure
that my baby is safe
in spite of my dread deed?

Please, help me
to forgive myself
and help my baby
to forgive me.

They say I should
believe that my baby
is now grown in you
and can pray for us.
Help me to know that
grace is coming even
out of my sin
because your love
covers a multitude of sins.

If there is a way
I can help other women
who seek abortion
as what seems to them
to be their only solution,
show me how.

Based on words of **Janet Krupnick**

A Prayer Affirming Life

God, you are the Lord and Creator of life.

You have blessed men and women
  with the privilege
  of bringing new life
  into the world.

You have imparted in our hearts
  the desire to nurture and protect life
  at all its stages.

I accept these gifts as a sacred trust.

Through the power of the Holy Spirit
  help me to affirm the value of life.

Grant me the wisdom and courage
  to speak out and defend human life.

Give me compassion
so that I may lovingly counsel
those who would reject the gift of life,
which is the reflection
of your image and likeness. Amen.

Women Affirming Life

Prayer for a Safe Birthing

My first child-birth!
O Mother Mary,
I'm so scared.

I don't want to go insane
with pain,
but I just can't believe
that I will be able to
do this natural birth
as gracefully
as all these women
who sound as if they never
even hurt at the dentist!

Of course, I'm willing
to go through
any amount of suffering
if only my baby
comes out safely.

Please, God, give me courage.
I offer up my future sufferings
for the good of my whole family.

Be with me Jesus, Mary, Joseph,
my guardian angel,
the baby's guardian angel,
and the doctor's also!

Anonymous

❧ After a Baby Is Born ❧

Once your very first baby is born, you probably have much more time to pray than at any other time of your life. Hours and hours are spent feeding baby, with cooing sounds going back and forth between baby and mother. What a wonderful opportunity for interspersing spontaneous prayers! Most mothers like to pray in gratitude for the beauty of their babies and also to beg God's protection.

Even though with subsequent babies you may have less time, you will benefit from continuing to express your needs in prayer quite a number of times during the day. This will help you to keep in mind that God, the holy family, the angels, and the saints are with you in all your joys and difficulties.

The following prayers address some of the specific

needs that can arise during this special time of your life and also suggest other possible subjects for prayer.

When a Baby Is Born

O God, our Father,
we give you thanks
for this little child
who has come to us from you.
Bless him (her) *now*
and through all the days of his (her) *life.*

Protect him (her) *in the days*
of his (her) *helplessness;*
bring him (her) *in safety through childhood's dangers;*
and grant that he (she) *may grow to adulthood*
and do a good day's work
and witness for you.

Help us his (her) *parents*
so to love him (her)
and so to train him (her)
that we will not fail
in the trust which you have given to us,

and that,
even as you have given him (her) *to us,*
we may give him (her)
back in dedication to you:
through Jesus Christ our Lord. Amen.

William Barclay
A Book of Everyday Prayer

Prayer on the Birth of the Baby

Alleluia
Alleluia
Alleluia

O, my God.
"My soul rejoices in God."
I never thought
I could love a tiny little creature so much.

Bless my baby
now and forever.
Make me a good mother.
Holy Mary, Mother of Jesus,
watch over us. Amen.

Prayer for a Baby with Birth Defects

God of Power and Might,
you could have so easily
healed my baby in the womb
if you had wished to.

Why did you let nature
take its course,
as if nature
were greater than you?

You know that I don't
always challenge you
with such questions.

*You know that most of
the time I am grateful
because you have shown
me the beauty of my baby's
personality
even if he (she)
is lacking in some features
most babies have.*

*God, I get so confused
when I read books
about children with
my baby's difficulties.*

*The experts seem to go so much
against my instincts,
with ideas about not
showing more love for
this baby because of
the problems.*

*Please send your
Holy Spirit
with wisdom from on
high about everything
to do with raising
this baby.*

*And I beg you, God,
to find some way
I can't see*

to lessen the pain
for my child
when he (she) has
to face attitudes of rejection
out in the world,
far from our loving family.

Now I entrust my baby
to you, Creator of all things,
knowing that in your eyes
this baby is especially lovable
because he (she) is destined for unusual sufferings
as was your Son.

Prayer for an Infant Who Died Suddenly

Oh God,
such grief!
How could you let it happen?

Didn't you know
how much I loved
that baby?

I want to believe
that our baby
is with you,
safe and sound.
And I do believe.
But I still can't accept it.

The pain is so great.
I remember his (her)
endearing little ways.
That smile.
That curly hair.
Those laughing eyes.

I even miss the
wailing in the night.
What wouldn't I give
to hear my baby
crying once again?

Please, please,
dear Jesus,
send me consolation.

I don't want to be
like those mothers
who refuse to ever
conceive again
because their pain
was so great.

I offer you all
the agony of my heart,
begging you to help
me by sending me
the incredible faith I need
to live through
this year of misery.
Jesus, crucified on the cross,

I am dying next to you.
Tell me,
as you did
the good thief
that one day
I will be with you
in paradise
and my baby, too.

Prayer of a Mother Who Adopted a Child

God, I ask your blessings
on that woman,
the natural mother of my child,
who loved enough
to bear her child
knowing that she would not
be able to take care of him (her)
after the birthing.

I realize there must always be an
ache in her heart
for that child
who now is mine.

Sometimes I look at my baby's face
and I wonder about
those traits that never
were shown in my family.

Take away any fear in my heart
so that my baby may drink
in the security of our love.

Thank you, Jesus,
for adopting all of us
into your holy family.

Based on the words of **Janet Krupnick**

Prayer for a Baby to Be Given in Adoption

In a way,
you, God the Father,
gave up your Son
for adoption
into the hands of
St. Joseph.

Be with me
at this time
when I am seeking
the right parents
for the baby
I can't take care of.

Be with me
at the moment
I have to let my baby
out of my hands

into the waiting
hands of strangers.

God,
you alone,
know how much
I love this baby.
How much I wish
I could keep him (her).

Anonymous

Prayer of a Mother with a Babe at the Breast

This prayer was inspired by St. Francis de Sales, who said that God wants to give us his love as much as a mother needs to let her babe relieve the heaviness of the milk in her breasts.

Come quickly, dear baby.
Suck the milk
that awaits you
in my overflowing breast.

There now,
you are at peace
and I am at peace.

So, too, does our God
long for us to come
to the waters

of his loving heart.

That we may be at peace
and he finds one to receive
his overflowing love.

Prayer for a Care-giver

Jesus, it was not my plan to work
when my baby was so small.
Yet, when I prayed for a way to stay home
no way seemed possible.

So, as I reluctantly leave my darling
with a child care-giver
I thank you for the love
for my baby I see in her eyes.

May my baby soak in that love.
May he (she) not feel abandoned.
Let me be thankful to you, God,
for providing another woman
with a desire to nurture
little babies.
Let me be happy to give her
the money she needs
to continue with her life.

May the guardian angels of
the babies in the care-giver's
home surround and protect
the children. Amen.

Anonymous

Prayer of the Infant's Care-giver

They bring my children every day,
the mothers on their way to work.
They go because they must.
They kiss their young, "Bye Bye, Baby, I love you."
Then they go. Because they must—or think they must.
Some mornings their hearts break.
Some mornings they are flooded with relief,
"It was an awful night, he (she) wouldn't let me sleep."
They go.

I stay.
I do what women have always done.
In their thousand ways the babies plead:
  "Feed me. Hold me. Love me. Watch me.
  Heal me. Change me. Know me. Love me.
  Love me. Love me. NOW!"
I give them what I have.

That evening the mothers come.
The children turn from me,
their tiny bodies squirm with joy,

"My Mama's here.
Now let me Go!
My mother's here."

Empty at the end of the day, I pray,
"Thank you, Lord, for these new lives.
Bless them, Lord, keep them safe.
    Bring them back to me.
Bless their mothers, too.
Clear from the mother's heart the day's debris.
Let them know that there will always be another job,
    another class.
But, Lord, please let them see that there will never
    be another day when their child
    will be exactly as he (she) is today.

As they hold their babies let them know not
    just their own burdens and weariness,
But, Lord, let them know the unspeakable
    common miracle—
That as Mary was chosen to give her bone
    and flesh and heart to the Infant God
They, too, have been chosen,
    to bring your love once again into the world."

Lord, bless us, the mothers and me.
Make us worthy of these new lives.

Rebecca Geraghty

Prayer of Thanksgiving

Thank you, God,
for my baby being healthy today;
for the doctors and nurses (and midwife)
who helped bring my baby safely into the world;
for the beauty of my baby's face and body;
for the love for the baby
coming from the whole family;
for another day to love my baby.

Grace Geist

Prayer for a Sick Baby

Jesus, once a mere babe,
have mercy on my poor sick baby.

Why does such an innocent little darling
have to suffer so much?

Perhaps I will never know the answer,
but I can still beg you to lessen the pain
and take away my fear.

I offer you my fear
and beg you to send me prudence
in the treatment of the illness.

When I am anxious
may your love flow through me
as I try to comfort my baby.

I pray that one day
this baby and I
and all our family
may be in the place
where there is no pain
and no tears
as you promised us.

Prayer While Changing Diapers

O God,
sometimes in my simplicity
I question why you invented
such wretched processes
as the digestive system
that led to the need for
these endless unpleasant
diaper changings.

Help me to understand
your will in creating
us with bodies of so
complicated but necessary
a design.

Help me to praise you
for the body of my baby

so beautiful
if so helpless
and smelly.

Lead me to offer
the unpleasant side
of my daily tasks
for a good life
for my baby on earth
and a blessed one
in heaven
in the perfect
Resurrected Body
that will be a gift
given to the blessed.

Prayer for the Spirit of a Good Servant

Dear God,
you know how little most of us
learn of the spirit of service
in our selfish world.

Now I am called
to serve this little beloved baby
twenty-four hours a day.

I feel overwhelmed.
Sometimes my joy overcomes all fatigue

but sometimes I feel so burdened
I can hardly stand it.

Send me your grace
so that I may want
to perform all the tiny services
my baby needs so evidently.

Send me also
lots of help
from family members,
friends,
and others,
that I may not
feel too isolated.

❧ Prayers for the Spiritual ❧ Welfare of the Baby

We mothers have all kinds of hopes and desires for our newborns. Chief among them is our prayer that each child, from the very first days and weeks of life, will flourish and grow in the Lord. Here are a few prayers that specifically address some aspects of the spiritual well-being of our infants.

Prayer before Baptism

O my Jesus,
I am so eager
that my little one
receive his (her) first kiss

as you take away
the stain of original sin
and enfold my baby
into the community
of your mystical body.

May this great moment
be a time of grace
for our whole family
especially those who have
drifted away from your sacraments.

May my promise
be sincere and permanent
when I join the others
in repudiating Satan
and all his works
so that I may cling
to you, my Jesus,
forever and ever. Amen.

Consecration Prayer

To the Immaculate Heart of Mary
and the Sacred Heart of Jesus
and to the Protection of the Angels.

Before the court of heaven
I, the mother of (name),
offer to you
my newborn child.

I ask that you would always
protect him (her)
and bring
special graces
so that all of his (her) *life*

he (she) *may walk*
in your paths
with the virtues
you have blessed
guarded by his (her) *own angels*
and all the angels

and that one day
my baby
may be a fully mature saint
who will dwell
in heaven forever.

Anonymous

Prayer for Healing of All That Prevents the Mother from Loving her Baby

I come before you, Creator God,
with a feeling of shame.

I wanted to love each baby
unconditionally
but I find
in my heart
there are certain obstacles to loving this one.

You know how much I wanted a girl (boy).
That may seem ridiculous
but it is true just the same.
Help me to be delighted in the sex of this baby
because it was your will that our baby be a boy (a girl).
Heal in me whatever made me partial to one sex
over the other
especially attitudes deeply buried in my family.

Why am I comparing this baby with
another of our children?
I realize that each baby
is unique,
but there is something resistant
in me
that would have liked a clone
of my other baby.

I feel so confused by these emotions.
I have learned that only you, Lord,
know how to bring peace and new life
when I am agitated
by irrational feelings and thoughts.

Give me a vision
of the special beauty
of this child
and the place
he (she)
will occupy in my heart
so that my love
may grow
to be as perfect as yours.

Sometimes the obstacles to the spiritual and emotional well-being of our children are present not just in us, their mothers, but also in other members of the family. The following prayer asks God to overcome these obstacles by sending his cleansing, protecting Spirit into the entire family.

Prayer for Healing of the Family Tree

God, the Father, almighty
Creator of all beings,
it is you who decided
that the human race
should be formed into families.

We know that since the fall
of our original parents
our family ancestry includes
not only talents and virtues
but also much tragedy and sin.

Today, reflecting on the legacy
of our families to my little baby,
I ask that you would heal our family tree.

I call to mind each member of the family
I have heard of
or known personally
and I ask for your healing
graces to bless him (her).

We know that in you, eternal God,
all of time is one,
and so we ask you
to bring the light
of your Son's redemption
into the darkness of the past.

Especially, I beg you,
loving God,
to cleanse me
of any bad patterns
coming from my family background,
so that my love
will be a source
of good for my
beloved child.

Our sister, St. Clare of Assisi
used to say that
"Our body is not made of iron.
Our strength is not that of stone.
Live and hope in the Lord,
and let your service be according to reason.
Modify your holocaust with the salt of prudence."

Come, O Holy Spirit,
to teach us how to mingle necessary sacrifice
with proper self-love,
that we may be able to respond
to the needs of our babies
in ways that are prudent and sound.

Chapter Four ❧

Prayers for Mothers of Young Children

This delightful Scottish poem by Alexander Anderson (1845-1909) captures something of the frustration and fulfillment experienced by mothers of young children everywhere. While not a prayer, this excerpt of "Cuddle Doon" (as the poem is titled) depicts a mother's love and prayerful concern for all her restless brood.

The bairnies cuddle doon at night
With mirth that's dear to me;
But soon the big world's trouble an' care
Will quiet doon their glee.
Yet, come what will to each of them,
May He who rules aboon [above]
Aye whisper...
"Oh, bairnies, cuddle doon!"

Alexander Anderson[1]

Many are the concerns of mothers of small children and of school age children. It is my hope that this chapter will help you find ways to lift up your worries to the Lord, giving you comfort and access to God's grace.

This chapter is designed mainly for mothers of preschool and grade school children. Thus, the first part addresses concerns of mothers of very little children in the home; the second part contains prayers for mothers of older children who are venturing out into the world of streets and schools. As I have not aimed to arrange these prayers into strict categories, however, there is some overlap. Also, you may find that you can relate to quite a number of the prayers presented here—whether or not your children fall into these age groups!

Of course, even as we are praying *for* our children, we mothers will be praying *with* them—introducing the children themselves to simple prayers such as the sign of the cross, the Our Father, the Hail Mary, and spontaneous prayers of petition and thanksgiving.

❧ Blessing Prayers ❧

The Sign of the Cross

Many mothers have a custom of blessing their children by making the sign of the cross on their foreheads, with or without holy water or holy oil. A mother might sign her children in this way as they leave the house or go off to bed, and also before long or dangerous trips.

Consecrations

In the Catholic Church there is a long tradition of consecrating children to Jesus or Mary in the name of some revelation such as the Sacred Heart of Jesus or the Immaculate Heart of Mary. The last chapter presented a simple consecration prayer for a newborn. Here is another consecration that a mother could recite over her child, or even have the young one recite.

Act of Consecration to the Most Sacred Hearts of Jesus and Mary

Most Sacred Hearts of Jesus and Mary, I consecrate myself and my whole family to you. We consecrate to you: our very being and all our life. All that we are. All that we have and all that we love. To you we give our bodies, our hearts and our souls. To you we dedicate our home and our country. Mindful of this consecration, we

*now promise you to live the Christian way by the practice
of Christian virtues without regard for human respect. O
most Sacred Heart of Jesus and Mary, accept our humble
confidence and this act of consecration by which we
entrust ourselves and all our family to you. In you, we
put all our hope and we shall never be confounded. Most
Sacred Heart of Jesus, have mercy on us! Immaculate
Heart of Mary, be our salvation!*

Praying with Candles

A blessed candle that is lit and then remains shining
for a time can be a lovely form of prayer, reminding us
that Jesus is the light of the world (John 8:12). A mother
might express her prayer in this way, particularly when a
child is sick or afraid. A simple prayer for these occa-
sions is, *"Lord Jesus, light of the world, be a light to my
child,* (name)."

Many mothers like to light such candles in church as
a symbol of prayers lifted up for their children. (When
you light candles at home, make sure to use safe candles
inserted in holders to avoid tipping!)

It is a lovely tradition to keep the baptismal candle of
each child to be rekindled on his or her feast days and
holidays such as Christmas and Easter.

Invoking the Aid of Patron Saints and Guardian Angels

Many times during the day a mother can invoke the aid of the baptismal saint of a child or of other favorite saints by praying, quite simply: "(Name of saint), *please intercede for dear* (name of child)."

Here is a litany to the angels that mothers can use in praying for their children:

Holy Seraphim, pray for us.
Holy Cherubim, pray for us.
Holy Thrones, pray for us.
Holy Dominations, pray for us.
Holy Powers, pray for us.
Holy Principalities, pray for us.
Holy Virtues, pray for us.
Archangels Michael, Gabriel, and Raphael, pray for us.
Holy Guardian Angels of (name each person in the family), *pray for us.*
Be our helpers by sending us light, protection, truth, guidance, and counsel.

Mothers can also teach their children how to pray to their own guardian angels. This traditional prayer can be used even with very young children:

Angel of God, my guardian dear, to whom his love commits me here, ever this day be at my side, to light and guard, to rule and guide. Amen.

Blessing with Holy Water

Holy water is what is called a sacramental: it is blessed and its use brings spiritual refreshment. Blessing oneself with holy water is suggested in times of danger such as fire, storms, and illness. It can also be sprinkled in a room or on a child to dispel the influences of the devil.

It is most customary to dip one's fingers in the holy water and to make the sign of the cross with the prayer, *"In the name of the Father, the Son, and the Holy Spirit."* Another recommended prayer is *"By this holy water and by your precious blood, wash away all my sins, O Lord."*

❧ Prayers for Trust ❧

Prayer of Mothers Who Are Afraid

Lord, protect the little fellows
with the giant feet
that find an obstacle in thinnest air
to tumble on

for I must take them places
that my skin has not touched first
and I'm afraid.

Lord, protect the little fellows
with their stubby limbs
that always catch the corners
at the cracks
for I must lead them forward
when my heart cries out "Go back!"
and I'm afraid.

Lord, protect the little fellows
with the shining eyes
that, brave and bold, so often
sink and swim
for I must take them outward
from the sunlight to the storm
and I'm afraid...

... and if my hand can't reach them,
if I falter,
if I fail,
if I stumble with them on the thinnest air,
then Lord protect the little fellows
keep them safe and sure,
Lord, protect my little ones
and lead them home.

Carla Conley Chervin

In the Time of Illness

O God, our Father,
bless and help (name)
in the illness which has come upon him (her).

Give him (her) *courage and patience,*
endurance and cheerfulness
to bear all weakness and all pain;
and give him (her) *a mind at rest,*
which will make his (her) *recovery all the quicker.*

Give to all doctors, surgeons and nurses
who attend him (her)
skill in their hands,
wisdom in their minds,
and gentleness and sympathy in their hearts.

Help us not to worry too much,
but to leave our loved one
in the hands of wise and skillful men (and women)
who have the gift of healing,
and in your hands.

Lord Jesus,
come to us and to our loved one
this day and at this time,
and show us that your healing touch
has never lost its ancient power.
This we ask for thy love's sake. Amen.

William Barclay
A Book of Everyday Prayer

Prayers for Single Mothers

Dear God,
I see you in the innocent face
   of my fatherless child.

I am afraid
   of all the things I cannot give
   of not being able to find the
   strength and the patience
   to perform this great task alone.

I have so much love, but sometimes
I feel so tired.

I call to you now in this rare quiet moment.
I will lean on you for comfort.
I will share these precious
   moments of watching my child grow.

With you to help
I am not alone.

Diana Chervin Jump

Mary, my mother,
and mother in heaven
of my children,
I give each of my children to you
one by one.

Now I have no anxiety
for I know they are in your
blessed hands
wrapped in your cloak.

I let them go
from my heart
into your heart.

Prayer for Trust in God

Dear God,
help us to realize that our children
are not just our children.
They happen to be yours.
They are yours first
before they are ours.
You love them much more than we do.
Your plans for them are surely better than ours.
The best way we can raise them up is to see to it
*   first that they know and love you, God,*
*   who is their true Father.*
If they are in your hands, God, what have we to fear?

Diana De Sola

❧ Prayers for Strength ❧ and Wisdom

Midday Prayers for Tired Mothers of Toddlers and Small Children

O God,
you see me here amidst my brood
so tired, stressed out, ready to scream.

I offer you these feelings
and beg you to receive them
as a sacrifice
for my dear little ones,
your dear little ones,
that somehow my weariness
may be credit for them
for a good life
and for heaven.

Oh Patient God:
The dear nuns taught me that there are four reasons for prayer—to adore, to thank, to atone, to ask. Since none of them had ever been mothers they were probably not aware that, on occasion, there is another reason for prayer—to vent. I know you understand this type of

prayer comes to you phrased in anger, in humor, in melancholy, or even in borderline panic because it is usually a spur-of-the-moment, somewhat explosive kind of prayer needed to release built-up frustration without running the risk of offending our earthbound friends or relatives. Obviously, I am here with a venting prayer—Oh God, I am sooo sooo sooo tired of muddy feet, sticky fingers, runny noses, and BandAids—of dirty clothes trails leading to empty hampers—of LOUD flush funerals so soon after goldfish booths at parish carnivals. I am tired of waiting for the food folks who can make a combination of things like soybean oil and potassium sorbate taste like butter or corn oil and calcium sulfate taste like eggs to come up with fruits and vegetables that taste like hamburgers and fries. I am tired of being blamed for everything from one child's poor posture to another's lack of social involvement during recess… Lord, I guess I'm pretty much tired of everything that stains, spoils, plugs up, overheats, or needs batteries. AMEN. There, my heart is lighter now. As you know, dear God, venting prayers require nothing beyond love that listens. Thank you for being that kind of love for me and thank you, too, for making me a mother.

Lois Donahue

O Lord, help me.
I am so tired, so tired.
I love this little child,
but I am physically and emotionally worn out.
Infants are demanding—
late nights,
daybreak mornings,
unpredictable schedules.
I keep waiting for things to get back to normal,
only to realize this is now normal.
And I never dreamed how emotionally unstrung
I would feel.
I don't understand why the baby is crying.
The baby doesn't respond to me as a person.
I'm depressed.
I feel alone.
Calm me, Lord.
This will end soon.
Schedules will emerge.
Baby will sleep longer.
I will be more energetic.
I can find satisfactions
if not in meaningful coos and smiles
then in the warmth of a baby close to me,
needing me.
I can seek relief—
go shopping some evening,
share my feelings with my husband,

call friends who are glad to listen or talk awhile,
call the doctor to ask all my "little" questions,
(I have been too proud to admit I don't know)
and I can snatch
every spare moment of rest possible.
Help me relax as I realize
an infant is more than smiles, rosy cheeks,
and affectionate sounds.
But a child, a new baby, is a miracle—
new, ongoing life in your creation.
Thank you.

Judith Mattison
Adapted from *Delight in the Gift*

Parent's Prayer

They are only little once, Lord.
Grant me the wisdom and patience
to teach them
to follow in your footsteps
and prepare them
for what is to come.

They are only little once, Lord.
Make me take the time to play pretend,
to read or tell a story;
to cuddle.

Don't let me for one minute
think anything is more important

than the school play,
the recital,
the big game,
fishing, or the quiet walk hand in hand.

All too soon,
Lord,
they will grow away
and there is no turning back.
Let me have my memories with no regrets.

Please help me to be a good parent, Lord.
When I must discipline,
let me do it in love,
let me be firm, but fair;
let me correct and explain with patience.

They are growing away, Lord.
While I have the chance
let me do my best for them.
For the rest of our lives,
please, Lord,
let me be their very best friend.

Mary L. Robbins

Prayer for Help in Raising Small Children

Jesus, Mary, Joseph,
you are the Holy Family.
I place our family in your hands.

*Some days I feel so tired, worn out, and discouraged
I wonder if I can stand being a full-time mother.
I want to throw them all into a day-care center
and work at anything, just to get away from the
constant crying, bickering, and boring household chores.*

*And yet I feel so called to witness
to the possibility of being a mother at home
who is a nest for her children
not a harried career Mom.*

*I don't really want a substitute for myself
in the form of a child care worker
or a mother whose own children come first.
Yet you see how much I need relief.
Please send me a way to get some help
and some rest each day*

*— a part-time nursery?
— a part-time helper
and the money to pay her
from somewhere?*

Grace Geist

❧ Prayers for Love ❧ and Selflessness

Prayer for Siblings of a New Baby

Dear God,
it is by your creative love
that we have families
with more than one child.

My heart is aching
for the jealousy
I know my born children
feel at the thought of another rival.

Help me to develop love in them
for this new child who will love
each of them so much.

Give me added energy
so that the birth of the new one
will not take all my strength
but that I will have plenty
to show my love for each older child
each day.

Diana De Sola

Prayers to Love Each Child

Father, I thank you for all my children.
You have given them all to me to love,
*   care for and raise for your purposes.*
Grant me the grace to love each one of them
*   the way you want me to love them.*
Grant me the faithfulness to take care of all their needs.
Grant me the wisdom to lead them to your plans for
*   their lives.*
Grant me a deep joy for being their mother. Amen.

Anonymous

Loving Father:
*   Your words, "for the Lord of all shows no partiality,"*
and your example of a father not partial to any of us, his
children, taught me something very important about
being a parent. As a mother of children who are individ-
ually unique, who have different gifts depending on the
role you created them to play, who are as human as I am
human and who will most likely hurt me as I have hurt
you, I needed to learn that my root love for each of my
children must be like yours—without preference. It was
you who helped me do that and I will be forever grateful.
*   What saddens me though, dear God, is that I feel my*
children, especially my growing-up children, do not
believe my love is impartial. When I scold one of them or
demand obedience, they forget I did the same to their
brothers and sisters. When I give time or attention to
another, they don't remember when they were ill, or

unhappy or in any way doing battle with life. That's when I see the hurt in their eyes—a feeling of being neglected or a longing for affection—and my heart aches. I lie in bed later wondering if any one of them had an equally or, worse yet, a more demanding need of which I was not aware. But, oh God, I have only two arms for hugging, only one lap for holding, only two hands for helping and only one demand-cluttered mind with which to make moment-to-moment decisions as to who or what must take priority. Regretfully too, I am often a weary mother, an uncertain mother, an impatient mother.

So again I come to you in prayer, asking that you help me be a better mother and help my beloved children to somehow understand that my heart, like all true mothers' hearts, can only love in equal parts.

Lois Donahue

Prayer to Love Each Child in an Individual Way

*Help me to understand
each of my children
in his or her uniqueness
and not always to compare
them to each other.*

*Let me see each one's personality
taking form under your hand, God,
and my own task as lovingly to affirm
the process you are letting take place.*

Diana De Sola

Prayer to Overcome Possessiveness

Dear God,
as I look at my wonderful child
I want to keep him (her) *small*
so that I can love and protect him (her).

Help me to realize that my child
is more your child than mine.

Help me to let go enough
so that my child can become his (her) *true self*
and not a clone of myself.

Help me to be grateful
for those little signs
that someday he (she) *will be independent*
such as reaching out in love
to someone else besides myself,
or having interests I do not share,
or wanting more time alone.

My God, what could be greater than your love,
and yet you express it in giving us freedom.
May my child one day be able to say
I am still close to my mother even as an adult
because she let me be myself.

Maureen McCarthy

Prayer of Repentance

Heavenly Father, forgive me for my impatience,
   unkindness, and selfishness towards my children.
Forgive me for making them meet my own standards
   instead of yours.
Teach me, Father, to humbly seek your will for each one
   of them.
I surrender to you my plans for their lives.
And Lord, make me patient, kind and loving toward them.
Teach me better ways to express my love to them.
Help me, Father. Amen.

Grace Geist

❧ Prayers Based on Sayings ❧ of Women Saints

St. Teresa of Avila wrote: *"Christ has nobody now on earth but you, no hands but yours, no feet but yours; yours are the eyes through which Christ's compassion looks out at the world, yours are the feet with which he is to go about doing good, and yours are the hands with which he is to bless us now."*

St. Teresa of Avila,
Doctor of the Church,
teach me how to understand my daily work
with my small children in this light
—not as tedious chores to finish at last,
but as a ministry of love,
lived in Christ's grace,
toward my dear little ones.

"Don't be discouraged if you do not see the good you do," wrote Venerable Thecla Merlo, foundress of the Daughters of St. Paul. *"Most of the time people are helped through obscurity, hidden sacrifices, instead of the fervor of a clamorous apostolate. Above all, let us try to lay aside our own ego, for this is what ruins everything."*

Dear Jesus,
help me to be happy to be doing so many things
for my children that no one sees or praises,
offering up the loss of the ego-gratification
of public achievement for the sake
of blessings for my family.

To the sisters in her convent, St. Rafaela Maria (a modern Italian saint) once wrote: *"Take good care of yourself... have a good appetite. God does not want his spouses to look as though he fed them on lizards."*

Pray for us mothers,
St. Rafaela,
that we may listen also to your good advice
and not get so worn down by our care for our little ones
that we become weak and exhausted.

Little Thérèse of Lisieux,
you said that nothing was small in the eyes of God
and that we should do many little things with great love.
Please intercede for me
that I may always remember the great worth
of my millions of daily acts of love
for my small children.
Let me never grow discouraged
because no one seems to value these works,
since it is Jesus whose eyes I seek
and his eyes shine with joy
when I give love to my children.

St. Catherine of Genoa,
help us to know as you did
that if it were given a person
to see virtue's reward in the next world,

*we would occupy our "intellect, memory and will
in nothing but good works,
unconcerned about danger and fatigue."*

Mother Teresa of Calcutta likes to say:

*At the end of life we will not be judged by
how many diplomas we have received
how much money we have made
how many great things we have done.*

*We will be judged by
"I was hungry and you gave me to eat
I was naked and you clothed me
I was homeless and you took me in."
Hungry not only for bread—but hungry for love
Naked not only for clothing—but naked of human dignity
and respect
Homeless not only for want of a room of bricks—but
homeless because of rejection.
This is Christ in distressing disguise.*

*Dear Jesus, help us mothers of small children to realize
how much you value our daily sacrifices for our little ones,
that we become not too overburdened and discouraged.*

❧ Prayers for a ❧ Child's Growth

Prayer for Growth in Learning

Lord, may my child like Daniel show
aptitude for every kind of learning,
(be) well informed,
quick to understand
and qualified to serve... (Daniel 1:4).

May he (she)
speak with wisdom and tact,
and may he (she) be
found to have a keen mind
and knowledge and
understanding and also the ability...
to solve difficult problems (Daniel 2:14; 5:12).

Lord, endow my child with
wisdom and very great insight,
and a breadth of understanding
as measureless as the sand
on the seashore (1 Kings 4:29).

Quin Sherrer and **Ruthanne Garlock**
Adapted from *The Spiritual Warrior's Prayer Guide*

Prayer for Virtues

Jesus, teacher of virtue,
help me to know how to encourage
my children
to be generous,
pure-minded,
eager to know those of other ethnic groups,
patient with their siblings,
orderly in their habits.

I ask you for these graces
not just so that my life may be peaceful
but because I love these virtues
myself.
May I always be able to model virtue
for my children
no matter how great the temptation
to give way to an easier path.

❧ Prayers for Protection ❧

Prayer for Safety in the Neighborhood

Lord, Jesus,
you know how much I care about
the safety of my children,

and you also know that
we don't have the money
to move to a place
with security guards.

I don't want to be overly anxious
so that my children can't have any fun
except in the house.

And so, I ask you to send your angels
not only to watch over my children
but also over all the children in our town (city).

Diana De Sola

Prayer for Good Friends for My Children

Lord, I am so grateful for my children's friends.
Thank you for each one of them.
I pray that I may never allow my children
    to play with children who would be bad for them
Just because they might be attractive or wealthy or
    intelligent
When they lack the goodness that means so much more.
Please send the friends to my children you want for them.

Prayer for Sitters

Mother Mary,
if I lived in Nazareth
in your time,
would you, perhaps, have been my sitter?
I ask you to pray for the ones to whom
    I entrust my children
that they may be as loving and careful
as you would have been,
and also as prayerful.
I especially ask that they be protected
from any form of neglect or abuse.
May God give abundant grace to the sitters
in reward for their services.

Grace Geist

Prayer for a Latch-key Child

Mother Mary,
you know
I didn't want
my children
to come from school
to an empty home.

But, here I am,
a single mother,
who has to work
til five o'clock.

When my children
come through the door
at three o'clock,
will you be there
for them,
Mother Mary?

If we pray
the rosary each evening
will you still be there
in the room
when they return from school?

Will you send your spouse,
the Holy Spirit,
to direct my children
to good things
to do each afternoon?

Please.

Prayer for Good Mentors for Our Children

Lord, I come to you today confused.
You know I want the best for my children.
I don't really know which school to choose for them.
I don't know whether to stay in my parish
where some of the teaching is not as Catholic as it should be,

or to go to another parish
far from my children's friends.
I am not sure whether to enroll my children
in the usual extracurricular activities
for fear they will make friends
with boys and girls
who later may not be good influences on them.

Even at home I feel confused.
Should I ban the TV completely
to safeguard my children
from bad programs
or should I monitor them myself
using time I need for chores
to sit and discuss the programs with them?

Please, Lord, send your Holy Spirit
to help me decide,
and send me good Catholic friends
who can give me wise advice.

Send special blessings on our priests,
teachers, and community leaders
so that they will be able to mentor my children well.

Diana De Sola

❧ Prayers for Special Times ❧

When a Child Goes to School

O God, our Father,
our child is going to school for the first time today;
and we cannot help being anxious
at this first step away from home.

Keep him (her) safe from all that would hurt him (her)
in body or harm him (her) in mind.

Help him (her) to be happy at school,
and to know the joy of learning
and playing together with other boys and girls.

Help him (her) to learn well
that he (she) may grow up to stand on his (her) own feet,
to earn his (her) own living,
and to serve you and his (her) fellowmen;
through Jesus Christ our Lord. Amen.

William Barclay
A Book of Everyday Prayer

Prayer for a Young Person Having to Confront a Death[2]

Dear Jesus,
you wept when Lazarus died even though you knew
that you would bring him eternal life.
You wept for the loss to his sisters and friends on earth.
I ask you to send soothing comfort to my child
facing the painful and shocking death of a loved person.

Help me to find ways to let my child express his or her
feelings about this death—bewilderment, anger, fear
about this death and about other possible deaths even
more fearful....

Let me not force my child to repress grief
because I don't want him (her) to be depressed.
Show me how to talk about the one who died
and to model the reality of spiritual presence to my child
in my prayerful communion with him (her).

Give me the right words to help my child to believe
that the loss of the physical presence of the beloved one
does not mean this one is not still spiritually present.
Help my child to know that he (she) will see (name)
again in your eternity.

Let this experience of death lead to a deeper understanding
that the unique personhood of the one who died
is a greater reality than his (her) physical being.
May he (she) know that we cannot lose
one who has become part of us through love.

One day we will all live with you,
Jesus, Mary, and Joseph
in our eternal home.
May I show my child how to live grief
in the light of the sure hope of eternal life.

Before Going on a Vacation

O God, Our Father,
we thank you
for this time of rest
from our daily work
and our daily business.

We thank you for time to spend with our family
and in the circle of those most dear.
We thank you for the open road,
and the hills and the seashore,
and for the clean wind on our faces.
We thank you for games to play,
for new places to see,
new people to meet,
new things to do.
Grant that the days of our holiday
may refresh us in body and in mind,
so that we may come back
to work the better,

because we rested awhile;
through Jesus Christ our Lord. Amen.

William Barclay
A Book of Everyday Prayer

Prayer for Driving

God our Father,
you led Abraham from his home
and guarded him in all his wanderings.
You guided him safely to the destination
you had chosen for him.

Be with us now as we travel.
Be our safety every mile of the way.

Make us attentive, cautious and
concerned about our fellow travelers.
Make our highways safe
and keep us from all danger.

Guide us to our destination for today
and may it bring us one day closer
to our final destination with you.
We pray this in Jesus' name. Amen.

Sacred Heart Auto League

Prayer for a Good First Confession and First Holy Communion

My Lord,
as my child is being prepared
for these two great sacraments
I ask you to bless our whole family
with a special love for these gifts
that we may manifest their power
in our own conversion,
in our own growth in holy love.

Please bless my child's teacher
with special graces of your Spirit
so that he (she) *may*
enkindle in my child
a deep love
for your presence
in the sacrament of forgiveness
and the sacrament of Holy Communion.

Diana De Sola

❧ Prayers for Youth Based ❧ on Writings of Women Saints

Dealing with youth takes qualities different from taking care of small children. This insight of St. Madeleine Sophie Barat (French foundress of an order of sisters dedicated to education) seems relevant for mothers today:

> "It shows weakness of mind to hold too much to the beaten track through fear of innovations. Times change and to keep up with them, we must modify our methods."

St. Madeleine Sophie,
show us how to be loyal
to the truth in old customs
but open to new possibilities,
for we want only to help our children
and not to impede their progress
through stubbornness,
but also not to experiment with their lives
by over-enthusiasm for new theories.

The founder of an educational order, Blessed Marie Rose Durocher, said this prayer that many a mother may want to echo:

"Give me the spirit you want them (the children) *to have."*

Concerning the death of one of her young children, St. Elizabeth Seton wrote to her friend: "It would be too selfish in us to have wished her inexpressible sufferings prolonged and her secure bliss deferred for our longer possession... though in her I have lost the little friend of my heart."

St. Elizabeth Seton,
we ask you to come to comfort
the hearts of mothers grieving
for children who died in youth.
Help us to believe in the eternal life of our child,
a life incredibly richer than the one left behind.
Intercede for us that a lively faith
in reunion in eternity will overcome all despair.

To the young people in her charge St. Mary Mazzarello used to say: "Laugh and play and dash about as much as you like, only be careful not to say or do anything that would be displeasing to God."

May my child
live a life worthy of the Lord
and please you in every way:

bearing fruit in every good work,
growing in knowledge of God,

being strengthened with all power
according to your glorious might

so that (child's name)
may have great endurance and patience,
and joyfully give thanks to the Father,

who has qualified him (her)
to share in the inheritance of the saints
in the kingdom of light.

For he has rescued (child's name)
from the dominion of darkness
and brought him (her) *into the kingdom*
of the Son he loves,

in whom (child's name) *has redemption,*
the forgiveness of sins (Colossians 1:10-14).

Quin Sherrer and **Ruthanne Garlock**
Adapted from *The Spiritual Warrior's Prayer Guide*

Dear God,
by no means did you make most young people
to be quiet and sedate.
I pray you to open my heart
that I might rejoice
in the high spirits
of my children
instead of trying to repress them
for my own peace of mind.

Chapter Five ❧

Prayers for Mothers of Teenagers

Lord, I never knew I visited you in prison.
I've never been in a prison.
I was imprisoned inside a twelve-year-old body
that was exploding with so many emotions
that I no longer knew who I was
and you loved me into being myself.
I was imprisoned behind my teenage rebellion,
my anger, and my stereo set,
and you came and sat by the wall of my hostility,
took the abuse I heaped upon you,
and waited in love for me to open the door.

Patsy Pollock

M any mothers imagine falsely that they will have no difficulty with their children during the teen years. Trouble is unthinkable, they assume, because they have brought up their children in such a Christian manner (unlike other mothers in the neighborhood!) But this view fails to take account of some important factors: the sins and imperfections of even the best parents and children, the pressures and temptations of the world in which we live, and also the mysterious workings of God's grace.

My guess is that this chapter will be very relevant for most mothers. If, however, you are a mother who is experiencing no difficulties with her teenagers, praise the Lord for his goodness and skip this chapter—or pass on the appropriate prayers to friends who may be in need of them!

❧ Prayers for Trust in ❧
Times of Anxiety

O God,
you know how worried and anxious I am about (name).
Help me to be sensible
and to see that worrying about things
does not make them any better.

Help me to be trustful,
and to do all that I can,
and then to leave the rest to you.

William Barclay
A Book of Everyday Prayer

Prayer for a Daughter Entering Teen Years

Dear God,
Now my sweet winsome girl is
entering into the tempestuous sea of the world.
I am so afraid that she will change
from being her own self
to becoming a copy of everything
that goes under the name of teenager in our culture.

I realize that I cannot save her
from going through the process of being a teen,
but my heart is full of anxiety for her.

*Please give me strength to trust
that the good qualities of my daughter
may sustain her through this trial.*

*And if she thinks she has to experiment
with anti-Christian values,
may I be the one she trusts to trust
that she will emerge one day in a blossomed true self.*

Prayer for Trust in the Spirit of God

*I will not worry, fret or be unhappy over you.
I will not be anxious concerning you.
I will not be afraid for you.
I will not blame you, criticize you or condemn you.*

*I will remember first, last and always
that you are God's child,
that you have his Spirit in you.
I will trust this Spirit to take care of you,
to be a light to your path,
to provide for your needs.
I will think of you always,
as surrounded by God's loving presence,
as being enfolded in his protecting care,
as being kept safe and secure in him.*

*I will be patient with you,
I will have confidence in you,
I will stand by in faith*

and bless you in my prayers,
knowing that you are growing,
knowing that you are finding the help you need.

Anonymous

Sometimes despite the mother's love, hopes, and prayers just expressed, a child does not seem to grow in the Lord. Realizing that many children do meet disaster, at least as far as we can tell, I have written these lines to add to the above prayer:

Even if you seem to perish
from the standpoint
of what I can see on this earth,
I will believe that God will save you
in ways I cannot imagine.
"I will always bless you" (Genesis 12:2).

Prayer for a Teen in Despair

My God, my God, why have you abandoned him (her)?
You hear my teenage child
praying for hope
in the midst of such depression and despair.
I am terrified
that the darkness will overtake
my child.

Come with your light
into that darkness
and restore my child
to joy in life.

And if my child
has swum so far out on the ocean of melancholy
that no one can reach him (her)
I pray for a special grace
to know without doubt
that you were there to save him (her)
even after he (she)
took his (her) *life,*
for nothing is impossible for you
and your mercy endures forever. Amen.

Prayer for the First Day a Teen Drives Alone

Terror!
O Jesus!
You know how badly my teen drives,
even though passing the driving test!
And you know what's out there:
drunken drivers,
drive-by shootings,
druggies,
other teen drivers!
Help!

Please send your guardian angel
to help my teen drive that car.
Send me a spirit of trust
that I may believe
that even if my teen
has an accident
you are with (name)
and that all is in your hands.

❧ Prayers for Growth ❧

Prayer for Growth in Wisdom
and to Do Well in School

Save me, Lord,
from the temptation
of wanting my teen to succeed
just for worldly glory
or a justification of my own pride.

May my teen never believe
that I think success in grades
is more important than growth in wisdom.

Yet I believe I should pray
that my teen do well
if in this way
he (she) *will have more chance*

later to serve you as a Christian in the world
or as one consecrated to serving you in the Church.

Please give me wisdom
so that I can encourage my teen
in the directions
that are truly your will. Amen.

Grace Geist

Prayer for the Gifts of the Holy Spirit in Confirmation

Pour forth your gifts
of wisdom,
counsel,
understanding,
courage,
teaching,
of tongues,
interpretation of tongues,
of prophecy,
of healing
and miracles.

May no Catholic,
especially these young people
being instructed for Confirmation
in our Church,
go forth to meet

the world, the flesh, and the devil
without a rich store
of the gifts of your Spirit.

Anonymous

Graduation Prayer

I am proud of (name).
There he (she) is in the procession
and I am glad that with all the teen dropouts
of our time,
my child made it to graduation.
Now my thoughts turn to the future.
O God, please give my child
an opportunity for work
that will be good
not in the eyes of the world
but in your eyes, Lord.
And if you want him (her) to go on for further studies
give us the resources
and give my child the desire
and the perseverance. Amen.

❧ Prayers for Patience ❧ and Acceptance

Prayer to St. Monica

St. Monica—
I turn to you as one who understands.
It seems like nothing I do is ever right,
that every attempt I make is met with opposition.

I look to you for guidance in raising my rebellious child.
Help me to see a light at the end of the tunnel.
Help me see that all my struggles are not in vain.
Give me patience not only with my son/daughter,
but with myself as well.

I hope to have the courage as you had, St. Monica,
to accept the will of God
in my child's life and continue to trust
in God's divine providence.

Scott Connolly

Prayer to Be an Affirmer

Come, Holy Spirit,
to remind me of
what I was like as a teen.
As I recall how different
I was then from the way I am now

I feel contrite for the harsh way
I sometimes judge my teenager
and the way my harshness
makes him (her) feel that I have no hope.

I need your help, Spirit of truth,
to see the good qualities of my teen child.
Focus my eyes to see those qualities in action.
Show me how to affirm him (her)
in ways that will reach to the heart.
Let the sun never set on my anger.
Amen.

❧ Prayers for Special Needs ❧

Prayer for Employment for a Teen

Not another summer of a teen
lounging about the house
with nothing to do,
please, Lord.

You know how the devil makes work for idle hands.
I beg you to send angels
to guide my teen
to a place
of wholesome work

for pay or volunteer
so that this time
may be one of growth
and maturity
not of regression
and boredom.

Diana De Sola

Prayer for Modesty in Teen Children

Dear Mary,
conceived without sin,
pray for our family
that we may have the courage
to dress and act in modest ways
so as not to become a source
of temptation to others.

I ask especially that my daughter
be given confidence in her own natural gifts
so that she doesn't need to flaunt her sexual attractiveness
in a desperate desire for popularity.

Help sons to realize that giving so much attention
to young women who display their sexuality in a bad way
saddens the chaste young women
who want to follow Christian teaching.

Give my teenage child (children)
great trust that you will call them

to the vocation in life
that will bring them
the greatest fulfillment
as women and men of your Kingdom.

Diana De Sola

Prayer for a Daughter's First Period

Dear Mary,
my daughter, (name), is now a woman.
But she still seems like a child.
In your day,
girls were engaged
right after their first period.
I entrust to you,
Mother Mary,
all the years of my daughter's bleeding
in preparation for conceptions.
Give her the grace to accept the discomfort and pain,
in the light of the glory of her womanhood,
and also,
if she be called to the single or consecrated life,
that she may see her period
as a sign of her spiritual motherhood,
as from the bleeding wounds of Christ,
came all our graces.

Prayer for Good Friends for a Teen

Lord, I ask you to send my son (daughter)
friends that will be both fun to be with
but also good companions.

You know how much my child
wants to find a true friend
and how ready he (she) may be
to grab hold of any friend
who likes him (her)
even if that teenager
is not on your path, Lord.

If the friends my teenager
has found are not good
would you please either
take them away
or
change their hearts
so that they will follow your ways?

I ask you especially to keep my teen
away from any friends who are addicted to bad ways
such as gang members to violence
or groups that indulge in fast driving,
drink, drugs, or sex.

Please help them to find good Christian friends
who love your ways.

❧ Prayers Based on Thoughts ❧ of Women Saints

St. Frances Cabrini wrote, "Did a Magdalene, a Paul, a Constantine, an Augustine, become mountains of ice after their conversion? Quite the contrary. We should never have had these prodigies of conversion and marvelous holiness if they had not changed the flames of human passion into volcanos of immense love of God."

And so we ask you, St. Frances Cabrini,
to beg Jesus to send special graces
to teenage children of ours
who are on the wrong path,
that the passion of their sins
may become the dark backdrop
for the fire of the love
for their Redeemer
they will one day experience.

St. Angela Merici, an Italian teacher born in the fifteenth century, wrote to her disciples: "You will effect more by kind words and a courteous manner than by anger or sharp rebuke, which should never be used but in necessity."

My God, what challenging words!
I try to be patient with my teenage children,
but then when they defy me openly
I burst into anger and sarcasm.
I realize that only divine grace
can bring patient and firm loving kindness
free from uncontrolled anger.
I ask you, Holy Spirit,
to direct me to the counsel I need
from friends or professionals
so that I may learn
how to deal with teen disobedience
in the right way.

St. Thérèse of Lisieux had this to say about the mercy of God: "If the greatest sinner on earth should repent at the moment of death, and draw his last breath in an act of love; neither the many graces he had abused, nor the many sins he had committed would stand in his way. Our Lord would receive him into his mercy."

O my Jesus,
you see into the heart of this mother,
so stricken with sorrow
and wrenched with fear
about her teenage child
whose path has so much
deviated from yours.

*You know how much I want to see
my child back on the right road,
your road.
I renounce my passionate desire
to see the conversion
of my child right away,
and ask instead only
to be given a complete trust
in the final salvation of* (name),
my child, and your beloved.

❧ Prayers for ❧ Troubled Teens

Teenagers searching for independence can present special challenges to parents. One minute, your home may be flooded with sweetness and light. The next, storms of frustration and rebellion threaten to overwhelm everyone and everything in its path. At times like this, you may feel like a toy sailboat in a stormy ocean. And when you do, the words of the psalmist, as recorded in Psalm 107, may offer you a source of consolation and hope:

*Those who go down to the sea in ships
Who do business on great waters;
They have seen the works of the Lord,
And His wonders in the deep.*

For He spoke and raised up a stormy wind,
Which lifted up the waves of the sea. . . .
Then they cried to the Lord in their trouble,
And He brought them out of their distresses.
He caused the storm to be still,
So that the waves of the sea were hushed.
Then they were glad because they were quiet;
So He guided them to their desired haven.
Let them give thanks to the Lord for His lovingkindness,
And for His wonders to the sons of men!
Let them extol Him also in the congregation of the people,
And praise Him at the seat of the elders.

Psalm 107:23-32

Prayer for a Son Growing into Manhood

*Oh Lord, my heart aches so for this child of mine, this
nearly-man. He hurts so much, and I hurt with him. You
remember what it's like to be a teenager—and our Mother
knows the struggle in my heart to be wisely loving, and
how wisdom seems to come only after the event. I feel at
such a loss, Lord....*

*But I hear you gently whisper in my heart, "No, but I call
you to offer these very experiences to me, so that I in turn
may offer them to the Father.... Remember the words of*

my servant Paul, writing of his particular sufferings as 'completing what is lacking in Christ's afflictions.' You also, and your dear son, are in your turn becoming one with me as you offer these very pains and sorrows to me."

Dear Jesus, I thank you so much for this encouragement. I remember you want only good for us, even though the way can be so dark. The teenage years are so turbulent, Lord. We need your constant reminder to keep our eyes fixed firmly on you and your faithfulness.

So I hold up my beloved son to you anew, Jesus. I ask you to surround him and permeate every fibre of his being with the power of your love; let no part of him be untouched by your love, Jesus. I offer you all that he has been, all that has happened to him, all the experiences of his life, his hopes, his dreams, even those still hidden from him but lying deep within his heart. I hold up to you the young man that he now is, with all his distress, his pain, his anger, his confusion, his blindness, but also his love and generosity, his giftedness, his energy and vitality, his zest, which at the moment so often leads him into stormy waters. I ask you, Lord, to forgive him the outbursts of anger and frustration: He just doesn't understand all that is happening to him as he grows into manhood. Jesus, you know the end from the beginning, you alone know who he is to become, the man who will glorify your name.

Please knock at the door of his heart so that he can recognize it is you who are calling, and so open his heart and his life to you.

Sue Norris

Prayer for Teens under Temptation

Jesus, Mary, Joseph,
Guardian Angels of my teenage children,
they pretend to be so tough,
but you and I know
how weak and floundering they are.

I beg you to give them the grace to realize
that what attracts them so much in sin
is not the pleasure
but the fantasy of pleasure.

Send the Holy Spirit
to show them that sin
tastes stale the next day
so that they will not listen
to the lies of the Evil One.

And if they fail and fall,
please bring them back swiftly
to the haven of your forgiving love.

Helen Ross

❧ Prayers of Courage for Mothers ❧

Prayer to the Heart of God.

Oh, Lord,
You who know me intimately
Know, as I do, what a weak and broken vessel
I can be, I have been.
My sin clouds the way of virtue,
Leaves me stumbling on the straight and narrow path.
Show me how to walk uprightly. I will follow you.

Oh, Lord,
You who gave these kids to me
Know, as I do, how woefully inadequate
I can feel, I have felt.
Each day I measure my own shortcomings by the mile
And wonder if my children notice. They always do.
Teach me grace under pressure. I will trust in you.

Oh, Lord,
You who guide our family
Know, as I do, we often stray alarmingly
We do not listen, as we ought.
As you lead us by the cool and quiet waters.
We would rather run and frolic
than feel your rod and staff.
Gentle Shepherd, lead us still. Help us rest in you.

Heidi Hess

Prayer of a Mother of Homeschooled Teenagers

Lord Jesus, I thank you for the privilege of being able to educate our sons and daughters at home. Today I want to pray especially for our older children.

Thank you for the special relationship you have given us with each of them. Thank you for the gift of trust between us, that rebellion has not ruptured our mutual confidence. Help us to preserve this bond by a deep respect for their growing freedom and responsibility. Grant us wisdom and courage, so we will neither overprotect them, nor be afraid to set boundaries.

So much you have entrusted to us. There are times when I feel overwhelmed by the magnitude of our responsibility. Give us courage and strength in our weakness. Make up for all that is lacking in our efforts.

Give us parents all the guidance and help we need to give our sons and daughters true spiritual, moral, and intellectual formation. As we walk with them on the way to adulthood, we realize that we as parents have many limitations, and cannot provide all things for them. Already you have blessed us richly with many wonderful persons who are role models, tutors, coaches, and friends. Continue, Lord, to bless our children's lives this way.

Give them peers who walk with them on a path of virtue and goodness, rather than selfishness.

*Above all, Lord Jesus, I ask that you give them a true con -
version of heart. May their lives be governed by the deci -
sion to belong to you, and to accomplish your will. Amen.*

Pia Eva Crosby

Prayer of a Stepmother

Step-parenting is an inexact science, full of pitfalls and
promise. Developing a loving bond with your step-chil-
dren may be one of the greatest challenges you will ever
face. As your relationship with your husband's children
continues to grow, remember to nurture your mother's
heart by daily drawing near to the heart of the Father.
Ask Our Lady and St. Joseph to intercede for you, that
the Holy Spirit would give you special insight for the
task at hand.

*St. Joseph, pray for me.
You who raised the Son of God as your own
Help me to guide with a firm yet loving hand
These young lives that God has placed in my keeping.
When I do not get my way, or face resistance
May I be reminded of your patient heroism,
Of the overwhelming challenge you bravely met
In raising the Son of God.*

*Virgin Mary, pray for me.
You who faced the scorn and derision*

Of those who did not understand your task.
You who watched your Son follow His Father's will
Even when you were not privy to it.
You who bore it all, even the innocent torture
Of your only Son, without murmur or complaint,
Pray that I may patiently forbear when conflicts come.
Holy Spirit, give me strength.
You who enlivened the disciples at Pentecost
Remind me to bring these children's lives
Daily to the Father's throne in prayer.
You who moved on the face of the waters at Creation,
Move in my heart to make it soft and new.
Take away the hardness and pride that lurks within.
Give me the grace I need each day to be like Jesus.

Jesus, although you were never a father yourself,
You led your followers patiently, lovingly.
When they disobeyed you, still you forgave them.
When they would not listen, still you taught them.
When they ran away, still you drew them back to you.
Through it all, you loved them.
These children, as much as I love them, are not mine.
They are yours—give me wisdom to lead them to you.

Heavenly Father, how I need you!
Thank you that you have promised
Not to give me more than we can handle together.
Send your angels to guard and guide us.
May they protect us from both physical harm
And the arrows of disunity within our home.

Grant us peace in the face of trouble,
And thank you for your presence in our lives today.

Heidi Hess

Prayer for the Future of Our Children

"Be still, cease striving, and know that I am God" (Ps 46:20).

Lord, you have entrusted to us our precious children. You have allowed our love to co-operate with you, the creator of the universe, to bring them into this world.

You breathed your Holy Spirit into them at their baptism. You have renewed and strengthened them with your healing mercy at the sacrament of reconciliation. You unite yourself to them as life of their souls in the mystery of the Eucharist. Your Holy Spirit has come into their hearts with all your wonderful gifts at confirmation.

They have grown from infancy to being no longer children. They are on the road to adulthood, and yet what a long and difficult road it is. How vulnerable they are, as they are entering into a world so often hostile to truth and goodness, hostile to what is most precious in their souls: your own divine presence. How many trials and temptations face them, and we have to let go of their hands—they have to walk on their own.

*But you say to us, "Be not afraid, be still, and know that I
AM GOD." They are never really alone. You, O Lord, are
with them. Your healing mercy encompasses their inner-
most being, you are closer to them than they are to themselves.*

*Your infinite mercy works all things unto good for those
who love you. As we let go of the hands by which we were
allowed to lead them for so many years, we entrust them
even more to your infinite mercy. Amen.*

Pia Eva Crosby

✣ Prayers in Times of Tragedy ✣

A Prayer in Grief When a Teen
Leaves the Sacraments

*Lord, Jesus Christ,
how much I have always loved your sacraments.
With what patient love did I teach my child, (name),
to love you in them also.
And now (name) is simply throwing away
the sacrament of Holy Communion
and of Reconciliation
claiming that he (she) doesn't need these unreal crutches.
Only you, dear Jesus,
know the pain in my heart,*

and the fear for the future of (name).
I offer to you this suffering
and ask that each time it pierces my heart
you will save up my tears
in the chalice of your redemption
for graces to be poured out on my child
on the day
he (she) *is ready to receive them once more.*

Grace Geist

Prayer for a Teen Pregnant but Unwed

God,
Creator of all new life,
you know that I always taught my daughter
that she should never consider abortion
out of fear of my anger at her sinful activities.
I am moved that I was the first one she told.
But I am also unsure how to advise her.
I don't want to see her marry a boy
she would never marry otherwise.
I don't want to see her drop out of school
to be a single parent.
I don't want to raise the baby myself—
I've been through raising children so many times already.
I think it would be good
for her to offer the baby for adoption
but I am not sure about this either.

If you want me to help my teen
raise this baby, who is my grandchild,
give me good counsel how to work this out.
Meanwhile, I beg you to send
my daughter
special graces
to be strong enough to carry the baby to term
and not to give in to the temptation of abortion. Amen.

Prayer for an "Unwed Father"

St. Joseph,
I call upon you in this time of trial.
Even though you were innocent of sin,
you had to deal with the fear of
ridicule and worse
concerning the pregnancy of the woman you loved.
In the case of my son, (name),
I am not sure whether he should take his girlfriend
to himself as wife.
They are so young.
He says he loves her and wants the baby,
but I am not sure he knows what real love is.
I want to help the girl
with all the support
she needs to avoid abortion
but I do not know how far I should go
to avoid a situation of future dependency

that might last for many years.
Send your Holy Spirit
with special wisdom
for our whole family
during this time of crisis.

Prayer for a Runaway Teen

Gone!
My child is gone!
Forever?
Oh, no!
Is it our fault?
When will (name) *call us?*
Forgive me for anything I did or failed to do
which led to my teen's desperation.

Terrible images come to mind.
My beloved child
out on the streets
prey to every vice that is out there
and no one to protect him (her).
Jesus,
please inspire my teen to call us,
and let us be open to any kind of family counseling
that could help.
If he (she) *cannot come home,*
please have someone from a Christian center for teens
find him (her) *before it's too late.*

Jesus,
I give you my agonizing fear,
and ask that you give me incredible hope against hope
that you can save my teen
even if I cannot see it happening now. Amen.

Helen Ross

Prayer for a Teen Who Died

It's over.
Nothing I can do.
My dead child,
lying in the cold morgue.
I prayed that you would resurrect (name)
just as you raised Lazarus,
but you didn't answer me.

I want to be able to forgive
all those people
who were involved in this death
who caused it,
or who couldn't prevent it,
but I am having trouble
with my angry feelings.
Give me the grace to say as you did, my Jesus,
"Father, forgive them, they know not what they do."

Sometimes
I even feel angry with you

when I think that
you could have changed everything
so that my child
would not have died.

Yet
I realize
that only you can save my child in eternity.
Only you can bring us back together in the joy of heaven.
Like Mary,
I would hold
my child in my lap.
But even this has not been granted me.
Mary,
teach me how to hold my dead child
in my heart.
To give him (her)
to you to hold
until
we are all together again.

Diana De Sola

We are worried about our children, Lord.
They seem at times to be rebellious
and indifferent to you and your purposes.
We can't help but feel that we are to blame
when they take off on their precarious journeys
and flirt with those demons of darkness

that are capable of destroying their souls.

We know, O God, that our love for them
cannot coerce them into goodness
any more than your divine and eternal love
can compel us to follow you.
Maybe we are too absorbed in our own failures
and embarrassed by our inability
to lead them aright. Perhaps our love is selfish—
that we don't love them enough to let them go
even if we can't hold them back.

Help us, O God,
to love them as you love us,
patiently and perpetually,
whatever their decisions and actions.
And, though we cannot program their lives
to fit into our agenda for them,
help us to live in a way
that will lovingly influence them
and eventually draw them back to you.

Leslie and **Edith Brandt**
Draw Me

Chapter Six ❧

Prayers for Mothers of Adult Children

"He who binds to himself a joy
Does the winged life destroy;
But he who kisses the joy as it flies
Lives in eternity's sun rise." [1]

Lord, as I meditate on these words of the
poet William Blake,

Teach me how to let go of my
young adult children
trusting that my surrender
will be for their good
and that complete communion
will be in heaven.

I f you are the mother of adult children, you know that this season holds unique particular joys and challenges. There is the bittersweet experience of seeing sons and daughters leave home for marriage, career, schooling, or other reasons. We rejoice at their entry into adult life, yet we wonder: are they ready? Are they close to the Lord? Are they mature and strong enough to withstand the pressures of a perilous world?

We have so many hopes and dreams—and fears—for these adult children. We see that the problems and dangers they will now encounter are increasing in scope and gravity—just as our own direct influence in their lives is decreasing.

Yet a mother's love does not diminish over time or distance! Impelled by our loving concern, we can draw closer to God and learn to entrust our adult children more confidently to his care and mercy.

One final word about something that can be a particular obstacle to praying for our adult children: disappointment. Mothers may experience this for many reasons at this stage of life. Perhaps our children are rejecting what we taught them or struggling with problems we never expected. Perhaps our relationship with them is troubled and distant, not at all what we hoped it would be. Or maybe we are just growing weary of praying for situations that do not seem to change.

Whatever you are facing, it is my hope that the prayers in this chapter will help you persevere in bringing your children before the Lord. Take heart: He who called them into being is near them—and he hears the prayers of our motherly hearts.

❧ Prayers for Protection ❧

Prayer When an Adult Child Is Leaving Home

Dearest Jesus,
You gave me a mother's heart
and now I feel as if it is breaking.

My lovely twenty-year-old daughter
is ready to move out of our house.
I am tightly holding onto her
to keep her within heart's reach at least.

I should be pleased
that she is prepared to be an adult now.
Why has this left me feeling
like a lonely, sad child?

Please give me the gift of courage
to release her to your plans for her life.

No matter how much I love her,
you, Jesus, love her
so much more than I am able to.

You see down the road
all that her life holds for her
and I am only blinded by my tears and fears.

I ask for the gift to trust you.
She was a gift from you.
Help me to give her back to you.

I love you, (name),
and I choose to release
you to be all you can be.

Gently glance back at me....
Love,
Mom

Elaine Seonbuchner

Prayer for Chastity

Every day my adult child
has to face the temptations
of the world
in the marketplace,
in social gatherings,
in the circle of his (her) friends.

Mary,
Mother of Pure Love,
be a safeguard
to my adult child
and may he (she)
be a light to others
by the virtue of chastity. Amen.

Anonymous

❧ Prayers for Healing ❧

Prayer for Healing of Family Hurts

O, my Jesus,
when I picture my dear child, now an adult,
I can't help but be aware
of all the ways
(name) *goes forth into the world*
bearing the family wounds.
Heal him (her) *of the scars that come from these bad*
times of the past: (list painful problems of the family,
such as abuse, alcoholism, workaholism, sibling rivalry,
indifference, loss through separation or death, and
others you know of.)

Pour your soothing balm into those wounds
and bind my child to you with love
that he (she) *may be the one*
to start fresh
to bring great love from you into the world.

Diana De Sola

Prayer in Disappointment

Jesus, I wanted so much to see my child flourishing
with the talents I know are there.

Today, I have to realize
that he (she) is not traveling
on the path I chose.

Help me to believe
that you will meet him (her) on
the path he (she) has chosen.

Help me to avoid bitterness
and envy of those
whose children have succeeded
in ways I wanted mine to succeed.

Help me to let go of my dreams
and love what is good
in the dreams of my child
and to offer the pain in my heart
for the future you have in mind
for all of us.

❧ Prayers Based on the ❧ Psalms and the Saints

Many mothers at this age feel tired and discouraged. It can seem that all our youthful energies are spent, that the world is falling apart. Yet we can gain perspective by reflecting on the refreshingly relevant words of David in the Psalms, which provide a helpful springboard for prayer:

Bless the Lord, O my soul;
And all that is within me, bless his holy name.
Bless the Lord, O my soul;
And do not forget his benefits.
Who forgives all your iniquity,
Who heals all your diseases,
Who redeems your life from the Pit;
Who crowns you with steadfast love and mercy,
Who satisfies you with good for as long as you live
so that your youth is renewed like the eagle's.

Psalm 103:1-5

Help me, Lord,
to believe that you can renew me,
bring me fresh life in the Spirit.
Let me toss aside that worldly image
that I am over the hill
because my wrinkles are coming in.
Let me rejoice in you always

and at the same time
provide a witness
to my older children
that life doesn't end at fifty.

Prayers for Older Children Who Have Left the Sacraments

Eternal and merciful Father,
I give you thanks for the gift of your divine Son
who suffered, died, and rose for all mankind.

I thank you also for my Catholic faith
and ask your help
that I may grow
in fidelity
by prayer,
by works of charity and penance,
by reflection on your word,
and by regular participation
in the sacraments of penance and the Holy Eucharist.

You gave St. Monica
a spirit of selfless love
manifested in her constant
prayer for the conversion of her son Augustine.

Inspired by boundless confidence
in your power to move hearts,
and by the success of her prayer,

I ask the grace to
imitate her constancy
in my prayer for
(name) who no longer shares in the
intimate life of your Catholic family.

Grant through my prayer and witness,
that he (she/they)
may be open to the promptings of your Holy Spirit
to return to loving union with your people.

Grant also
that my prayer be ever hopeful
and that I may never judge another,
for you alone can read hearts.
I ask this through Christ our Lord. Amen.

Prayer of the Society of St. Monica

St. Mechthild of Magdeburg,[2]
you once wrote, "I was made of love...
therefore, in the nobility of my nature,
no creature can suffice me
and none open me, save Love alone."
Intercede for me as I am forced to let go
of my young adult children
to really know God's love as you did.

Blessed Juliana of Norwich,[3]
you once wrote that
"the reason we are not fully at ease
in heart and soul
is because we seek rest in these things
that are so little
and have no rest within them,
and pay no attention to our God,
who is Almighty, All-wise, All-good,
and the only real rest."
You see how little
at ease in heart and soul I am.
Please ask God to send me
that spirit of contemplation
you were given
so that I may be led to pay attention
more to God than to my worries.

During her time as a widow, Concepción Cabrera de Armida (more simply known as Conchita, a Mexican mother about to be beatified) experienced many graces of joy in the midst of the suffering of human losses. Let us meditate on her words and turn them into a prayer for mothers of young adults:

"Suddenly, when the soul is engulfed in pain, at these very moments, almost of despair, there comes a gentle breeze, changing parching arid suffering into a pleasant freshness without other desire than to please the Beloved, without dreaming any more about the pleasure of future goods."

In the face of fears,
disappointments and anxieties
about my young adult children
I turn to you, dear God,
and ask you to release me
from my wishes
for a good future on earth
for my progeny.

Give me instead
a foretaste of heaven
in the form of the
freshness of new life within my soul.
Instead of reveling in fantasies
about matters out of my control,
let me take my joy in you,
the source of all goodness.

❧ Prayers for Struggling ❧ Children

Prayer to Mary

Oh Mary, Mother of our Lord Jesus Christ,
you stood by in sorrowful prayer of love
as your son was condemned and crucified by the world.
The same sorrow that poured from your heart for your son,
I share for my children who
encounter personal conflicts
and despair in their own lives.
I pray for that same love of concern to be given
to my children
as they face the difficulties of the world.
Please give my children
the hope and love of God the Father,
that Jesus Christ promised on the cross.

Joseph Naill

Prayer of a Mother of a Single Adult Child

Dear Jesus,
beautiful love of all hearts.
You see my child, (name),
so lonely and uncertain.

I keep wishing that he (she)
would decide to be a consecrated priest (brother, sister)
to live totally for you and the kingdom.

Or, if that is not your holy will,
that you would send my son (daughter)
a wonderful spouse.

If you mean my child, instead,
to enjoy the freedom of spirit and of choices
of a single Christian in the world,
please give (name) peace about this state of life. Amen.

Grace Geist

Prayer for a Homosexual Adult Child

O my Jesus,
not this!
Watching other mothers dealing with the Cross
of a homosexual child
I thought I could do so much better!
I would have the compassion and wisdom
they seemed to lack.
But now when it is my child
I am in a panic,
especially from fear of AIDS.
I hear your voice
reminding me that
with you all things are possible.

You can heal him (her)
directly in a spiritual way
through the mentoring of a loving older person
or through a counselor.
You want me to bring this matter
to you in prayer
to beg for compassion
and to let you form
me into a loving parent
whose understanding
can be part of the healing,
even while I pray intensely
that my child be freed
from present sinful patterns
and from grave temptations to sin.

Helen De Sola

Prayer for an Adult Child with AIDS

Dear Jesus,
now the worst has happened.
Not only to have to give up
all my dreams for my child's future
but also to face his slow and painful death
of a shameful disease.
You who forgive everyone
I beg you to lead
my child into perfect repentance

to the sacrament of reconciliation,
to acceptance of the pain and death
he (she) *will face.*

I ask you to give me (and my husband)
so much love for our child
that our only wish
will be to pour this love out on him (her)
and not to spend hours in fruitless blame
or anger towards others who were involved.

For your mercy endures forever
and eternal life is the only life
that counts in the end.

Diana De Sola

❧ Prayers for Straying ❧
Children

Prayer to St. Monica

Dear St. Monica,
great intercessor for your son, Augustine,
the sinner who became a saint,
in remembrance of your many tears
when your son seemed lost,
I beg you to intercede for those of my adult children
who have strayed from the true path.

Beg Jesus to bring them safely
into the harbor of his Church
that the desperate sinful love they indulged for creatures
may be transformed into the burning love for God
of your son, St. Augustine.

Prayer for Fidelity to Christ in His Church

Mother Church,
call your children home.

I realize that they think the paths they have chosen
    are better,
but since, in fact, there is one true Church
founded on the apostles,
I long so much to see them in it.

I realize that they can be saved
by following the light that they see,
because you read hearts
and understand all the reasons
they do not turn to your Church
but they are missing so much joy and comfort
    and guidance
by having turned away.

Each day at Mass I offer them to you
and ask you to bless them
and bring them back yourself.
They won't listen to me! Amen.

Prayer for the Spiritual Welfare of My Child

Dear Jesus,

I wonder if my children still pray. I know they did when they were little because I heard their prayers, but now that they are grown, I wonder and I worry. Please help them to realize that prayer does change things—not just the wonderful, often miraculous, things that happen as the result of prayer, but what can change when they actually begin to pray. I fear that outside of prayer their faith, their belief in You, may waver because their minds cannot know You in the mystery of the Trinity. That's why I so want them to know that prayer brings "feeling" to their faith and lets their heart know You far more personally than their mind ever could. Please let them experience prayer becoming presence, Your presence. They so desperately need You present in their lives and to know that from You can be drawn whatever they might need to deal with the demands of day-to-day reality. I beg You, dear Jesus, guide my children to prayer.

Lois Donahue

❧ Prayers for Specific ❧ Blessings

Prayer for the Health and Economic Well-being of an Adult Child

God, source of all good gifts,
I know that holiness
is even more important
than health or wealth
but I come to you in prayer
in concern
about the well-being of my adult child.
He (she) is too old,
or often thinks so,
to take comfort
from me,
and so I ask that you send
your holy family,
Jesus, Mary and Joseph
to take care
of him (her)
and
to help (name)
to find good stable work
that will use the talents you have given
and also support the family. Amen.

Grace Geist

Prayer for the Future Spouse of a Daughter or Son

Dear Father God,
please send your Holy Spirit
in search of a good spouse
for my daughter (son).

I pray that this chosen one
may be full of love for you, God,
and one who accepts your Son, Jesus,
as his (her) *Savior.*

May the spouse of my adult child
be strong, good, loving and prudent.

Please give my child
the patience to wait
for the spouse you have chosen.

If she (he) *has impatiently*
gotten close in hurtful or sinful ways
to another man or woman
please heal and cleanse her (him)
of the wounds and stain
of those relationships.

Please give (name of adult child)
the gifts and virtues he (she) *needs*
to be a good spouse
for the one you have chosen.

Quin Sherrer and **Ruthanne Garlock**
Adapted from *The Spiritual Warrior's Prayer Guide*

Prayer for a Happy Marriage and Family

I know that it is wrong for parents
to mix into the problems of their adult children
in their marriages and childraising.

So, instead of nagging them
with good advice,
I will turn instead to you,
Holy Spirit,
and beg you to be with them even more
as they struggle through the problems
of marriage and children.

Teach them always to pray together as a family
and to seek from you fresh sources of love and strength.

And if there is some way I can help them
please show me how to do it
in a way that is not offensive or irritating. Amen.

Diana De Sola

Papal Prayer for Vocations

"Lord, Jesus Christ,
Good Shepherd of our souls
you know your sheep
and know how to reach man's heart,
open the minds and hearts
of those young people

who search for and await
a word of truth for their lives;
let them understand
that only in the mystery of your Incarnation
do they find full light;
arouse the courage of
those who know where to seek the truth,
but fear that what you ask
would be too demanding,
stir the hearts of those young people
who would follow you,
but who cannot overcome doubts and fears,
and who in the end follow other voices
and other paths which lead nowhere.

You who are the Word of the Father,
the Word which creates and saves,
the Word which enlightens and sustains hearts,
conquer with your Spirit
the resistance and delays of indecisive hearts;
arouse in those whom you call the courage of love's
answer:

'Here am I, send me!'" (Isaiah 6:8).

Pope John Paul II
September 8, 1992

Dear God:

So often I have prayed on behalf of my children—beseeching, begging, pleading. Thinking back, I feel there may have been times when I neglected to thank you for saying YES to those mother prayers. Please forgive me and let this be a cumulative "thank you," not only for the times I may have forgotten, but for all the times my prayers were answered in ways I never knew and especially for the times when you, with fatherly love, mercifully intervened in the lives of my children—times when I was not even aware they were in need of special prayer.

Lois Donahue

Chapter Seven ❧

Prayers for Grandmothers

As we watch our children raise *their* children, experiencing all the joys—and most of the frustrations—that we felt as parents, we discover the uniquely wonderful role that God has given us in these children's lives. As Jay Kesler observes in *Grandparenting*:

> We cannot spare them most of the struggles and failure of life. We can, however, demonstrate that after a long life filled with battles and victories, we can come out on the other side and do so with grace.[1]

Grandparenting brings its own challenges. Some women feel a certain emptiness because they have too little contact with their grandchildren (they live too far away, or because divorce or other family problems prevent frequent visits).

Other grandmothers feel "penned in" because they have *too much* contact. Some well-meaning women—wanting to help their children through difficult times—become so involved in caring for their grandchildren that they find themselves too busy to simply enjoy them.

The prayers in this chapter are for all grandmothers, reminding us of our most important task: to bring these little ones to Jesus in prayer, and to demonstrate to our grandchildren as best we can God's unfailing love.

Prayer to St. Anne
(patron saint of grandmothers)

Dear Lady Anne!

I know you must grow weary of hearing so often the same requests, but do be pleased to help my children to love and understand my grandchildren. I wasn't always terribly clever with mine when they were in need!

Ask Our Father to give them the grace to be better parents than I was, and me the grace I need to be a good grandmother. Amen.

Cecelia Walker

Grandmother's Thanksgiving

Thank you, God,
for each of my dear
little grandchildren

that I may love
without great burden,
watch with delight,
receive their tiny loving responses.

I thank you, God,
that you have given us
enough love in our family
so that visits are not
times of strife
but of mutual sharing
and content.

Help me to enjoy
being a secondary character
in the lives of my grandchildren,
not first, but still
very cherished.

Give my children
wisdom to bring them
up in a way
that will open
them to you.

Helen Ross

Prayer of a Lonely Grandmother

Dear Jesus,
I'd give all the pictures on my refrigerator
For just one hug from my grandson.
It seems so long
since the last time I held him.
Six months is a long time
in his four-year-old life.
Take my empty heart, heavenly Father,
and fill it up
with the joy of child's laughter.

Anonymous

Prayer for a Single Parent

So tired.
She is always so tired!
I wish her life wasn't so hard.

I know that she is better off unmarried
than in her previous situation
but it is hard to see her struggling alone
with so many problems.

God I ask you to send me grace
to be a good mother to her at this time.

Give me health so that I can be a comfort and help to her
and not an added burden.

Prayer of a Grandmother for a Sad Grandchild

Dear God,
look down tenderly on my dear grandchild.
You see how sweetly he (she) prays to you.

Things aren't so great at home just now for him (her).
I want him (her) to know that you are listening
and hovering over him (her).

Sometimes I can't hover
because that would be considered interference.
But you can interfere for my grandchild
and for all these little children
who live in a society
where there is violence in the streets,
violence in films,
not to mention
a diseased and much-too-used-up planet.

Lord, I want to picture you
hovering over all five billion of us.
Comfort them, love them,
make them feel safe and secure
in a very hostile world.
Make us all "get along."

Lord, be my grandchild's lifesaver.

Janet Krupnick

Prayer for the Grandmother of an Active Toddler

Sweet Jesus!
Where does he (she) *get*
all that energy?
I can't keep up
with that little boy (girl)!
The dog is hiding under the bed.
Grandpa is hiding in the basement.
I want to hide, too.
O Lord, please.
Isn't it almost naptime yet?

Anonymous

Prayer of a Grandmother in Thanks for a Grandson

Dear God,
Thank you for my new grandson.
I know I have a granddaughter already.
You know my gratitude for her.
But thank you especially
for this new grandson.
My son was adopted at five weeks
and I was so grateful then.
But this is really something,
arranging this new little boy for me.
It's as if you gave me those five weeks back.

I couldn't love my son more
with the five weeks or without.
But I am saying thank you for him
and I know he is deeply touched by this little boy.
I pray for my son's natural family.
I only wish they could somehow
share this joy with our family.
I love you, Jesus.
Thank you for coming to this earth
and letting all of us be adopted.

Janet Krupnick

Prayer to St. Hildegarde

St. Hildegarde,
intercede for me for my senior years
that I may grow in the graces that
led you to witness in these words:
"From my infancy until now,
in the seventieth year of my age,
my soul has always beheld this sight...
the brightness which I see is not limited by space
and is more brilliant
than the radiance around the sun...
sometimes when I see it,
all sadness and pain is lifted from me,
and I seem a simple girl again,
and an old woman no more."

Chapter Eight 🌿

Prayers for a Mother's Own Special Needs

And you shall nurse and be carried on her arm, and dandled on her knees. As a mother comforts her child, so I will comfort you.

Isaiah 66:12-13

T he motherly personality is inclined to pray constantly for spouse and children and neglect her own needs. But mothers need mothering too! For this reason it is especially important for us to let ourselves be loved by our God. Only as we know and receive this love for ourselves will we be able to dispense it to others. Also, turning to our Father, our Savior, the Holy Spirit, Mary, and the saints will bring a release from the temptation to turn our motherly concerns into subjects of constant worry.

❧ Prayers of Trust ❧

Do not fear what may happen to you tomorrow. The same Father who cares for you today will care for you tomorrow and every other day. Either he will shield you from suffering or he will give you unfailing strength to bear it. Be at peace, then, and put aside all anxious thoughts and imaginings.

Francis de Sales

Reminder

*The statues watched,
The candles burned
While all the pain poured out.*

*Tell me what to do.
Please, Lord, please.
I don't know what life's about.*

What about the job, the kids,
School and parents and sex and me?
Where can I find myself?

The simple answer comes each time,
Insisting to be heard,
"Trust me, Trust me."

To trust you is so simple, Lord,
Is that why it is,
So easy to forget?

Maureen McCarthy

Prayer

I looked for answers in the haze
of indecision
searched for ways
To find a clearing in the mist—
a guiding light—
a path I'd missed

The fog of questioning and doubt
Offered me no pathway out

I looked once more
in near despair
and there
was prayer

Lois Donahue

Dear Heavenly Father,

I remember one of my children saying to me, "Daddy has been frowning a lot. I sure wish he would smile. Things are always better when Daddy smiles." I told him his father was simply dealing with some temporary problems, that his daddy would be smiling again and that things would be better.

Now, thinking about wars and abuse and dissension in the Church—about crime and abortion and hate—my thoughts turn to you, dear Father in heaven, and the child in me prays that the frown-producing problems besieging your world will be temporary and that soon you will smile again because "Things are always better when Abba smiles."

Lois Donahue

Prayer in Economic Anxiety

Lord Jesus,
of the lilies of the field and birds of the air
you have taught me that
your love is infinitely
more important
than money and security.

But you surely know
how hard it is for us on earth
not to worry when the sources
of our income

become unsure
or seem to disappear!

I do not ask you for wealth
but to give me trust
to believe that our necessities
will be met
and that you will find us the employment
we need to take care of the family.

Blessed Mary, Mother of Jesus,
and St. Joseph, Foster Father of Jesus,
intercede for our family
in our time of insecurity.

Prayer to Overcome Fear of Economic Disaster

Dear St. Joseph,
you lived in times much more insecure than ours.
On your long journey to Egypt,
were you so sure that you would find
the work you needed to survive?

I bring to you my fear
that we will not have the work we need
to take care of ourselves
and our little ones.
Please quiet my fears
with a sense of the providence
of God the Father.

❧ Prayers Faith, Hope, and ❧ Love for Mothers

Act of Faith

O my God,
I firmly believe that you are one God
in three divine Persons,
Father, Son and Holy Spirit.
I believe that your divine Son became man,
died for our sins,
and that he will come to judge the living and the dead.
I believe these and all the truths
which the holy Catholic Church teaches,
because you have revealed them,
who can neither deceive nor be deceived. Amen.

Act of Hope

O my God,
relying on your almighty power
and infinite mercy and promises,
I hope to obtain pardon of my sins,
the help of your grace,
and life everlasting,
through the merits of Jesus Christ,
my Lord and Redeemer. Amen.

Act of Love

O my God,
I love you above all things,
with my whole heart and soul,
because you are all-good and worthy of all love.
I love my neighbor as myself for the love of you.
I forgive all who have injured me,
and ask pardon of all whom I have injured. Amen.

Increase the faith, hope, and love in my heart,
dear Lord,
so that I may be a better woman today.

❧ Prayers While Working ❧

Kitchen Prayer

Lord of all pots and pans and things,
since I've no time to be
a saint by doing lovely things
or watching late with Thee,

Or dreaming in the dawnlight
or storming heaven's gates
Make me a saint by getting meals
and washing up the plates.

Although I must have Martha's hands

I have a Mary's mind.
And when I black the boots and shoes
Thy sandals, Lord, I find.

I think of how they trod the earth,
at times I scrub the floor
Accept this meditation, Lord,
I haven't time for more.

Warm all the kitchen with Thy love,
and light it with Thy peace.
Forgive me all my worrying
and make my grumbling cease.

Thou who didst long
to give men food
in room or by the sea
Accept this service that I do,
I do it unto Thee.

Klara Munkres

Prayer to St. Joseph to Work in a Good Spirit

No doubt this prayer was composed originally for men working outside the home, but it is equally applicable to housework!

O Glorious St. Joseph,
model of all who are devoted to labor,
obtain for me the grace
to work in the spirit of penance
in expiation of my many sins;
to work conscientiously
by placing love of duty
above my inclinations;
to gratefully and joyously
deem it an honor to empty
and to develop by labor
the gifts I have received from God,
to work methodically, peacefully,
without ever shrinking from it
through weariness or difficulty,
to work, above all,
with purity of intentions and unselfishness,
having unceasingly
before my eyes
death and the account I have to render
of time lost, talents unused,
good not done,
and vain complacency in success,

so baneful to the work of God.
All for Jesus,
all for Mary,
all to imitate thee,
O Patriarch St. Joseph!
This shall be my motto for life and eternity. Amen.

Apostolate of Christian Action

❧ Prayers for a Positive Spirit ❧

When Angry

Today I come to you, Jesus,
full of anger,
peevishness,
irritability.

I wish that everyone in the family were different.
Why can't my husband be more like my best friend's?
Why can't my children be more grateful?

Jesus, I lay my head on your breast,
the way St. John did,
and ask you to soothe and comfort me.

Give me fresh energy,
fresh joy,
fresh gratitude,
fresh hope.

Prayer For Hope in Discouragement

The wish I have in my heart
is that you will be given by God,
daily throughout life,
one of His most precious gifts—
an ever-growing ability
to look beyond
every gray cloud,
dark night,
heavy cross,
upsetting situation,
or obnoxious behavior,
and see our Creator's hand
holding out to you
an opportunity to choose to think and act
in terms of faith,
hopefulness, patience and love,
instead of automatically reacting with
discouragement,
resentment,
hostility,
or complaints.

Your repeatedly manifesting
such a positive response
in the face of adversity
will spiritually enrich our world
by providing a model for the lives

of those blessed with the chance to know,
love and learn from you.
Wasn't it to teach us to fulfill this role with Him
that the Lord came to dwell among us?

James Gill, S.J.

Prayer for Cheerfulness

O God,
animate us to cheerfulness.
May we have a joyful sense of our blessings,
learn to look on the bright circumstances of our lot,
and maintain a perpetual contentedness.
Preserve us from despondency and from
yielding to dejection.
Teach us that nothing can hurt us
if with true loyalty of affection,
we keep Thy commandments
and take refuge in Thee.

William E. Channing

❧ Prayers for Special Times ❧

Prayer to Find a Home

Dear Mary,
I know that you had to travel
to a strange land
without knowing exactly
where your home would be.

Please intercede for me
as we start looking for the right place
to raise our little family.

It doesn't have to be fancy
but I so want it to be safe and not ugly.
Because I know you had a mother's heart
I place this request in your hands.

Also, please help me
not to be so upset about this time
of uncertainty.

Diana De Sola

Prayer for a Mother Whose Husband Has Left the Family

O my Jesus,
I feel so lonely,
frightened,
and bewildered.
I never thought I would be raising my children alone.

I cannot pretend to be happy
in the midst of this tragedy
but I need special grace
not to allow any bitterness
to poison my children's lives.

Give me a spirit of forgiving love
and patient hope
and may I receive your spousal love for me
in such abundance
that I may be able to overflow
with this love to my children.

May they love their father
in spite of everything
and may they find in the Fatherhood of God
a recompense for whatever is lacking
in their own father.

Please give us ways to meet our financial needs.
Send my husband a spirit of justice

to want to sustain the part of the support
my children need
in a steady, committed way.

Provide us, we beg you,
with the love of our extended family
and with many good Catholic friends.

Bless us all, dear Jesus,
now and forever, Amen.

Prayer in Menopause

My God,
Creator of my feminine body,
I feel strange coming into this new time.

I thought I would be delighted
to be rid of the pain and discomfort
of my period.
But now I am not so sure.
I feel old, finished.

I ask you to send me your Mother
and your women saints
to show me how to live this time
in a holy manner,

to show me how to become
more loving to my spouse,
more spiritually fertile,
and more motherly in the Spirit.

Diana De Sola

At the Loss of a Husband

My husband is gone.
I commend him into your hands.
I forgive him for everything
that he did that gave me sorrow.

Jesus, will you be my spouse?
You promise to love us
more tenderly than any husband
and you tell us that you
want our joy to be full.

I do not ask you to
take away suffering
that is good for me
at this time,
but I ask you
to give me hope
that indeed my joy will be full
if not here on earth
then in the eternity of eternities. Amen.

Prayer in a Time of Serious Illness

Lord Jesus Christ,
you who know my whole soul,
inside out,
you know that I am not afraid to die.
My fear is for my little ones.
They need me.
I have prayed and prayed for healing
and let others pray over me.
Nothing helps.
So now I commend myself into your hands
and beg that you would send your Mother
to take care of my children
and also to send others to help.
Give me a spirit of abandonment
to Divine Providence
and a belief that nothing is needed
but that your will be done. Amen.

Grace Geist

❧ Prayers for Mary's Help ❧

Dear Mary,
let me take shelter under your mantle,
so that I will not be so anxious.
I know that you are very generous to your children
for you love to give.
Help me this day to be like you.
Teach me how to make every room of my home
into an oratory.

Imitation of Mary

Let us walk like you through life,
Let us mirror you forever:
Strong and noble, meek and mild.
Peace and love be our endeavor.
Walk in us through our world,
Make it ready for the Lord.

Think in me, O Mother,
That my thoughts be clear and bright;
Speak in me, O Mother,
That my speech be true and right;
Work in me, O Mother,
My work is then well done;

Then holy is my labor,
My rest a holy one.
You penetrate my being,
Fill every part of me,
That all your ways and conduct
In me each one can see.

International Schoenstatt Center

❧ Prayers Based on Sayings ❧ of Women Saints

Come, Holy Spirit,
Help us to understand,
as did St. Syncletia,[1]
that we would be happy,
if we took as much pain to gain heaven
and please God
as those of the world do
to heap up riches.
Such worldly people
expose themselves to the fury
of winds and waves at sea,
and suffer shipwrecks and all perils.
They attempt all, dare all, hazard all.
But we in serving so great a Master

for so immense a good,
are afraid of every contradiction.
So let us not be so anxious
about every setback
and instead throwing ourselves
on the mercy of God
proceed courageously
to carry our crosses each day.

St. Perpetua,[2]
on the way to your martyrdom
you called out
that we are not in our own power,
but in the power of God.
Help me to believe
that I am in the power of God
so that I do not waste so much time
brooding about my own powerlessness.

St. Monica,[3]
you advised your friends
that they should guard their tongues
when their husbands were angry.
Let me confide in you.
I hate to have the children watch us fight,

and yet sometimes my husband's words
fill me with such anger
that I feel I would do violence
with my hands
if I didn't let it out with my tongue.
Please ask Holy Mary
to win for me the grace of a soft answer—
firm but lacking in sarcasm.
And show me how to be both assertive and humble
in ways that will bring about
greater love and harmony.

St. Catherine of Siena,
Doctor of the Church,
you wrote that no sin nor wrong
gives a person
such a foretaste of hell
in this life
as anger and impatience.
That's me all over.
I do not know how
to be less angry and impatient.
Please ask the Holy Spirit
to send me special insight
into the providence of God
so that I will not be so frustrated each day.

Blessed Juliana of Norwich,
you wrote that in heaven
we will experience great bliss
because we will receive
the Lord's own gratitude
for our good acts,
and all the blessed creatures in heaven
will see his thanking of us,
and that this joy will last forever.
I ask you to intercede for me
that I may get my mind off petty resentments
into the vision of this eternal happiness
so that I may be more serene and happy
in my daily life with my family.

St. Elizabeth Seton, writing about the tragic death of family members, proclaimed:

"What avails melancholy forebodings,
and indulgence of feeling
which can never alter the event of things?
One would, rather,
look at life's realities as they are
guided by a just and merciful Protector
who orders every occurrence
in its time and place...."

I know that these contradictory events
are permitted and guided
by thy wisdom which solely is light.
We are in darkness
and must be thankful
that our knowledge is not wanted [needed]
to perfect thy work."

Good Jesus,
take away my tendency to worry and brood
over wrongs of the past
and terrible possibilities of the future.
Give me the trust
you gave to St. Elizabeth Seton
that I may dwell in your peace.

"Let nothing trouble you, let nothing frighten
you. All things pass away, God never changes.
Patience obtains all things. Nothing is wanting to
one who possesses God. God alone suffices."

St. Térèsa of Avila

A prayer based on a meditation of St. Elizabeth Seton in a time of discouragement:

My Jesus,
I am so sick of myself.
I feel so weak
and so discouraged
by my failure to overcome
a single one of my humiliating faults.
I come to you
and lay the whole horrible list
at your feet,
reconciled by the graces of Confession,
and draw near again
to the fountain of your love
which is Holy Communion.
And now I feel refreshed,
strengthened
and ready to return
to the duties of my life.

Acknowledgements ❧

The compiler wishes to express her gratitude for the use of writings in common domain or with permission.

Nine prayers from William Barclay, *A Book of Everyday Prayer* (New York: Harper & Brothers, 1959).

Four prayers from *A Treasury of Prayers,* Catholics United for the Faith (New Rochelle, N.Y.).

Four prayers from Quin Sherrer and Ruthanne Garlock, *The Spiritual Warrior's Prayer Guide* (Ann Arbor, Mich.: Servant, 1992).

Two prayers from Leslie and Edith Brandt, *Draw Me* (Ann Arbor, Mich.: Servant, 1990).

One prayer from Judith Mattison, *Delight in the Gift* (Minneapolis, Minn.: Augsburg Fortress Press, 1990).

And prayers from these writers and groups: Rev. J. Alberione, Apostolate of Christian Action, Willian E. Channing, Scott Connolly, Diana De Sola, Helen De Sola, Lois Donahue, Grace Geist, Rebecca Geraghty, James Gill, S.J., Sister Angela Clare Gorman, S.P., International Schoenstatt Center, Diana Chervin Jump, Janet Krupnick, Daniel Lord, Maureen McCarthy, Joseph Cardinal Mindszenty, Klara Munkers, Joseph Naill, Pope John Paul II, Patsy Pollock, Mary Robbins, Helen Ross, Sacred Heart Auto League, Elaine Seonbuchner, Rita Snowden, Society of St. Monica, Cecelia Walker, Women Affirming Life, Rev. Luke Zimmer.

Bibliography ❧

Barclay, William. *A Book of Everyday Prayer*. New York: Harper & Brothers, 1959.

Brandt, Leslie and Edith. *Draw Me*. Ann Arbor, Mich.: Servant, 1990.

Catholic Prayer Book. Compiled by Msgr. Michael Buckley, Tony Castle, ed. Ann Arbor, Mich.: Servant, 1986.

Cook, Roy J. *One Hundred and One Famous Poems*. Chicago: Contemporary Books, 1958.

Duerk, Judith. *Circle of Stones: Woman's Journey to Herself*. San Diego: Lura Media, 1989.

Kesler, Jay. *Grandparenting: The Agony and the Ecstasy*. Ann Arbor, Mich.: Servant, 1993.

Leifeld, Wendy. *Mothers of the Saints*. Ann Arbor, Mich.: Servant, 1991.

Lord, Daniel. *Letters to My Lord*. New York: Herder & Herder, 1969.

Prayers for Daily and Occasional Use. Union City, N.J.: Passionist Missions, 1969.

Rojas, Carmen, ed. *Draw Me—Catholic Prayers for Every Occasion in a Woman's Life*. Ann Arbor, Mich.: Servant, 1990.

Seton, Elizabeth. *Selected Writings*. Ellin Kelly and Annabelle Melville, eds. Mahwah, N.J.: Paulist Press, 1987.

Sherrer, Quin, and **Garlock, Ruthanne.** *The Spiritual Warrior's Prayer Guide*. Ann Arbor, Mich.: Servant, 1992.

A Treasury of Prayers from Catholics United for the Faith. New Rochelle, N.Y.

When Someone You Love Dies, John F. Pearring, Jr., ed. Colorado Springs, Colo: The Catholic Herald, 1993.

Notes

Chapter One
Catholic Mother's Guide to Daily Spirituality

1. "Eternity" is taken from Poetry and Prose of William Blake, 1927, as found in John Bartlett, *Familiar Quotations* (Boston: Little, Brown & Co., 1855), 488.

Chapter Two
Mass as a Source of Spiritual Strength

1. The Mystical Mass prayer can be ordered as an attractive prayer leaflet from The Christian Renewal Center, 411 First St., Fillmore, CA 93015.

Chapter Four
Prayers for Mothers of Young Children

1. Adapted by David Benson in Roy J. Cook's *One Hundred and One Famous Poems*.

2. John F. Pearring, Jr. *When Someone You Love Dies,* (Colorado Springs, Colo.:The Catholic Herald, 1993).

Chapter Six
Prayers for Mothers of Adult Children

1. "Eternity" is taken from Poetry and Prose of William Blake, 1927, as found in John Bartlett, *Familiar Quotations* (Boston: Little, Brown & Co., 1855), 488.
2. St. Mechthild of Magdeburg is a medieval German Benedictine mystic.
3. Blessed Juliana of Norwich is a medieval English mystic.

Chapter Seven
Prayers for Grandmothers

1. Jay Kesler. *Grandparenting,* (Ann Arbor, Mich.:Servant 1993), 81.

Chapter Eight
Prayers for a Mother's Own Special Needs

1. First-century saint.
2. Early martyr.
3. Mother of Augustine.

Index of Prayers ❧
(by first line)